THE GROWTH OF THE ANTWERP MARKET
AND THE EUROPEAN ECONOMY

(fourteenth - sixteenth centuries)

III. GRAPHS

The Growth of the Antwerp Market and the European Economy

(fourteenth-sixteenth centuries)

HERMAN VAN DER WEE, LL. D., Dr. Hist.

Lecturer in Economic History, University of Louvain

III. GRAPHS

MARTINUS NIJHOFF, THE HAGUE, 1963

PRINTED IN BELGIUM

TABLE OF CONTENTS

PART I. **The economic growth in Antwerp and Europe expressed in graphs** **11**

Graph 1   Wheat prices in Brabant (1516-1590) 15
Graph 2   Wheat and rye prices in Flanders and Brabant (1460-1600). 16
Graph 3   Barley and oats prices in Brabant (1426-1550) 19
Graph 4   Prices of commercial articles, bought by several institutions of Brabant on the Antwerp St. Bavo's Fair (1426-1490) ... 20
Graph 5   Prices of tree-bark, barrel-herring and tallow-candles in pifferent Brabant towns (1506-1600) 23
Graph 6   Prices of wine-vinegar and peas in different Brabant towns (1427-1474).. 24
Graph 7   Official weight of fine silver in the groat of Brabant and Flanders (1363-1650) 27
Graph 8   Comparison between methods of trend-calculation of wheat prices 28
Graph 9   Correlation between wheat prices of Lier, Flanders and New Castile (1474-1545) 31
Graph 10   Frequency curve for summer day wages of masons in Antwerp from different sources (1456-1600) 32
Graph 11   Map of seignorial farms, property of the Poor Relief of Lier (c. 1560) and of the principal farms, property of Antwerp's St. Elisabeth's Hospital (c. 1560) 35
Graph 12   Map of farms, property of the Abbey of Tongerlo (fifteenth century) 36
Graph 13   Nominal rye prices in Antwerp and nominal wages in Brabant (1385-1439) 39
Graph 14   Nominal rye prices in Antwerp and nominal wages in Brabant (1410-1444) 40
Graph 15   Nominal prices and wages in Brabant (1430-1480) 43
Graph 16   Nominal prices and wages in Brabant (1472-1500) 44
Graph 17   Nominal prices and wages in Brabant (1489-1525) 47
Graph 18   Nominal prices and wages in Brabant (1517-1536) 48
Graph 19   Nominal prices in Brabant (1515-1555) 51
Graph 20   Nominal prices and wages in Brabant (1535-1555) 52
Graph 21   Nominal prices and wages in Brabant (1553-1573) 55
Graph 22   Nominal prices and wages in Brabant (1570-1590) 56
Graph 23   Nominal prices and wages in Brabant (1581-1600) 59
Graph 24   Statistics of production, commerce and immigration (1378-1620) 60
Graph 25   Number of apprentices received yearly into the Weavers' guild of Brussels (1417-1446) 63
Graph 26   Annual income from excise of Bergen-op-Zoom (1442-1555) 64
Graph 27   Hungarian copper exported by the Fuggers (1497-1539) ... 67
Graph 28   Annual income from rents of stalls and of shops belonging to the Church of Our Lady in Antwerp (1470-1581) 68
Graph 29   Rents in and round Antwerp and Lier (1440-1610) 71
Graph 30   Agricultural income in Brabant (1429-1620) 72
Graph 31   Annual comparison between real rye income of the Poor Relief of Lier and that due to it from the farmers (1480-1600) 75
Graph 32   Exchange rates in Bruges (1384-1412) 76

Graph 33 Exchange rates in Antwerp (1515-1600)   79
Graph 34 Interest rates for short term government loans in Bruges
          and Antwerp (1401-1570)   80
Graph 35 Interest rates for short term government loans on the
          Antwerp money market (1511-1555)   83
Graph 36 Number of poor families supported by the Poor Relief of
          Lier (1517-1597)   84
Graph 37 Expenditure, in percentages, by the Infirmary of the Bégui-
          nage in Lier on various foodstuffs (1526-1602)   87
Graph 38 Annual ducal income from the Cattle toll and Transport
          toll of Lier (1403-1648)   88
Graph 39 Comparison of trends of real income of wage-earners in
          Antwerp, Lier and Brussels (1382-1600)   91
Graph 40 Comparison of real income of wage-earners in Antwerp
          and Lier (1407-1600)   92
Graph 41 Yearly ratio between summer daily wages of mason and
          mason's labourer in Antwerp and Lier (1399-1600). Com-
          parison between the trends of rye prices and mason's daily
          wages in Antwerp (1390-1600)   95
Graph 42 Crisis behaviour of grain prices in Brabant (1403-1600) ...   96
Graph 43 Crisis behaviour of prices for meat and dairy produce in
          Brabant (1403-1600)   99
Graph 44 Crisis behaviour of prices for industrial crops in Brabant
          (1403-1600)   100
Graph 45 Crisis behaviour of industrial prices in Brabant (1403-1600)   103
Graph 46 Crisis behaviour of commercial prices in Brabant (1403-1600) 104
Graph 47 Crisis behaviour of transit trade, industrial production and
          the money market in Brabant (1403-1600)   107
Graph 48 Crisis behaviour of debts owned by farmers in Brabant
          (1497-1600)   108
Graph 49 Crisis behaviour of daily and price wages of skilled wage-
          earners in Brabant (1403-1600)   111
Graph 50 Crisis behaviour of daily and price wages of unskilled
          wage-earners in Brabant (1403-1600)   112
Graph 51 Trimestrial evolution of wheat prices, marriages and con-
          ceptions in Lier (1582-1600)   115
Graph 52 Comparison of price trends in Brabant (1391-1600)   116

PART II. Indices of volumes I and II   121

A. Index of persons and places   123
B. Index of subjects   143

VOLUME III

GRAPHS AND INDICES

PART I

THE ECONOMIC GROWTH IN ANTWERP AND EUROPE EXPRESSED IN GRAPHS

GRAPH 1

Wheat prices in Brabant (1516-1590). Averages per harvest year in Flemish money of account.

▬▬ Lier : according to the weekly bread weight.

.... Lier : according to the monthly sales of wheat by mills.

▬▬ Brussels : according to the weekly price lists (*Mercuriale*).

─── Lier : according to the weekly bread weight.

GRAPH 1

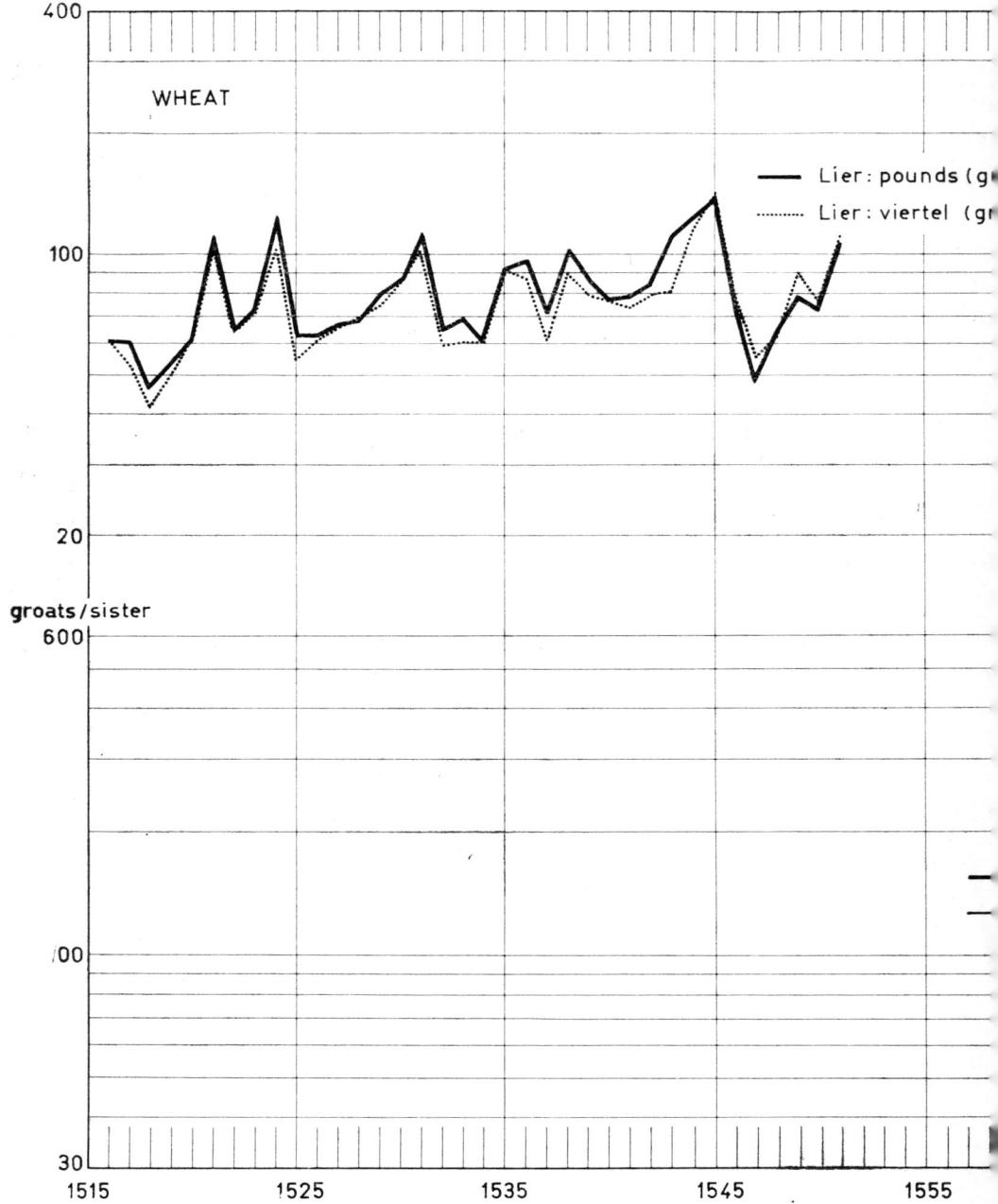

groats / pound

400

WHEAT

—— Lier : pounds (g
.... Lier : viertel (gr

100

20

groats/sister

600

/00

30
1515   1525   1535   1545   1555

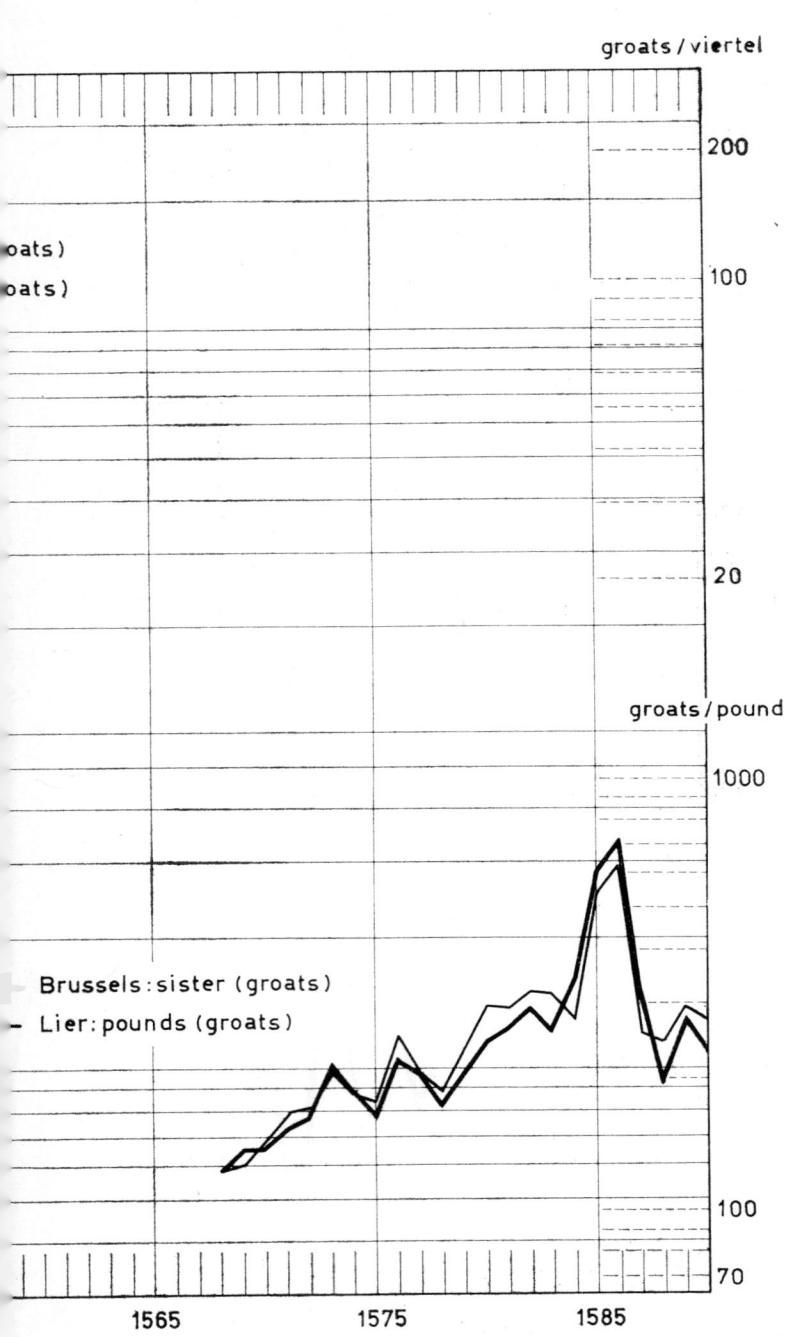

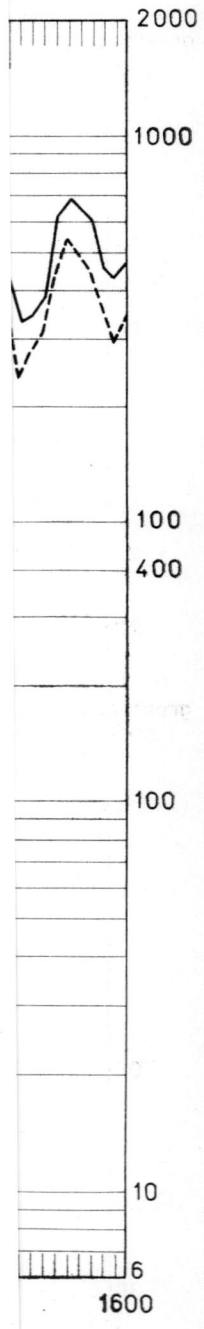

groats / viertel

200

100

20

groats / pound

1000

oats)
oats)

Brussels : sister (groats)
Lier: pounds (groats)

100

70

1565   1575   1585

2000

1000

100

400

100

10

6

1600

15

GRAPH 2

Wheat and rye prices in Flanders and Brabant (1460-1600). Averages per harvest year in Flemish money of account.
Wheat in Bruges per *hoed* (1564-1600) : ——— market prices
--------- count's annual price lists.

Rye in Brabant per Antwerp *viertel* (1460-1551) :
▬▬ Brussels (annual urban price lists)
.... Antwerp (annual ducal price list)
o–o–o–o Antwerp (St. Elisabeth's Hospital).

Rye in Brussels per *sister* :(1568-1590): ●–●–●–● weekly price lists (*Mercuriale*)
——— annual urban price lists.

17

GRAPH 3

Barley and oats prices in Brabant (1426-1550).
Averages per harvest year per Antwerp *viertel* in Flemish money of account.

GRAPH 3

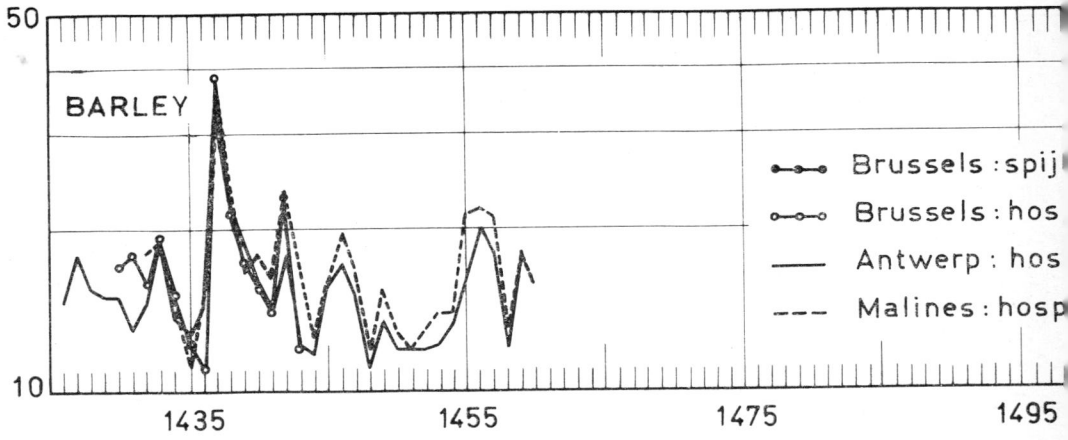

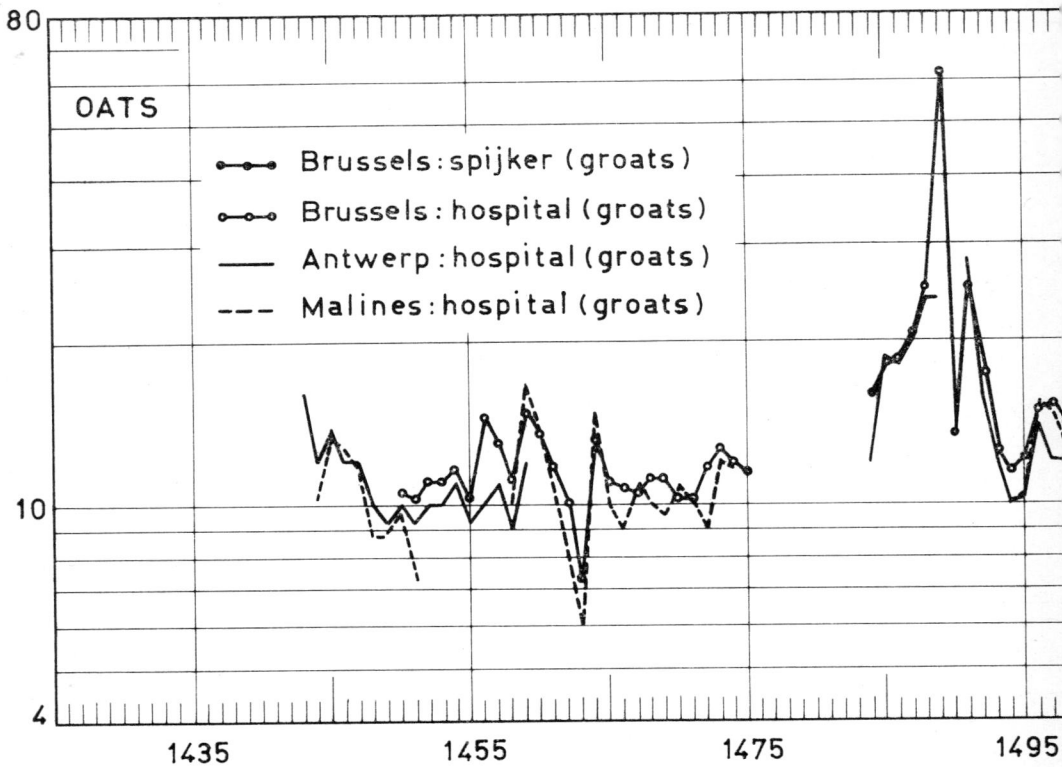

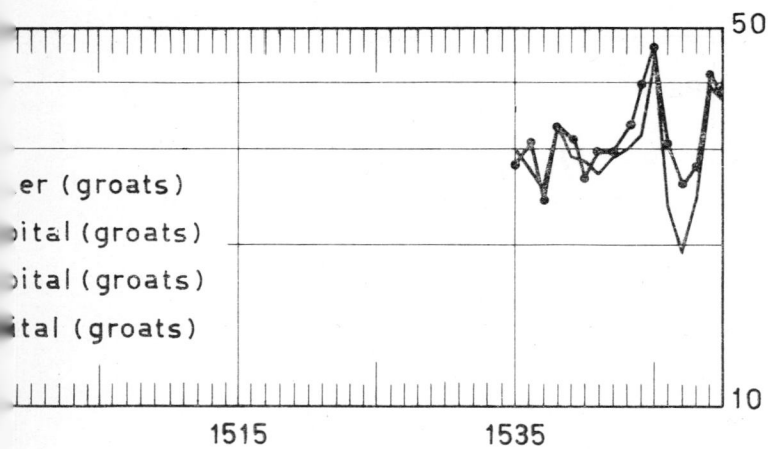

er (groats)
ɔital (groats)
ɔital (groats)
ital (groats)

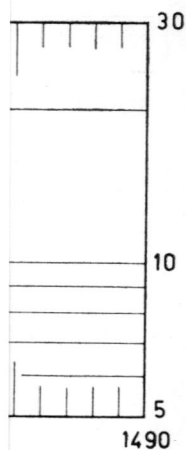

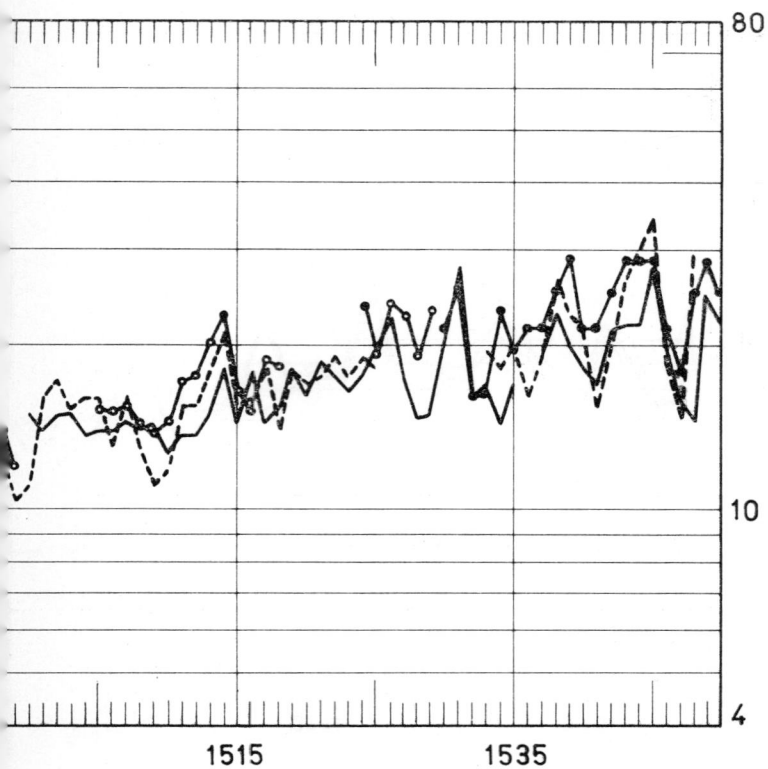

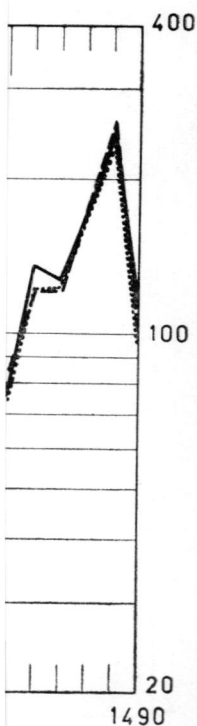

19

GRAPH 4

Prices of commercial articles, bought by several institutions of Brabant on the Antwerp St. Bavo's Fair, in Flemish money of account (1426-1490).
Pepper : per Antwerp *pound*
Flemish cheese : per Antwerp *wage*.

GRAPH 5

Prices of tree-bark, barrel-herring and tallow-candles in different Brabant towns in Flemish money of account (1506-1600).

Tree-bark : per *sister* of Lier
Barrel-herring : per Antwerp *ton* ([a])
Tallow-candles : per *steen* of Antwerp.

([a]) Exceptionally, the graph for the years 1531-1547 gives prices of purchases on the Antwerp market only, by institutions from different Brabant towns.

GRAPH 6

Prices of wine-vinegar and peas in different Brabant towns in Flemish money
of account (1427-1474).

Wine-vinegar : per Antwerp *ame*
Peas : per harvest year per *viertel* of Malines.

GRAPH 7

Official weight of fine silver in the groat of Brabant and Flanders (1363-1650).

26

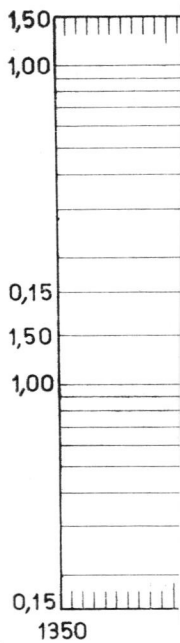

1350

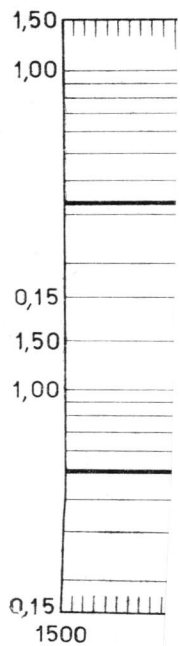

1500

GRAPH 8

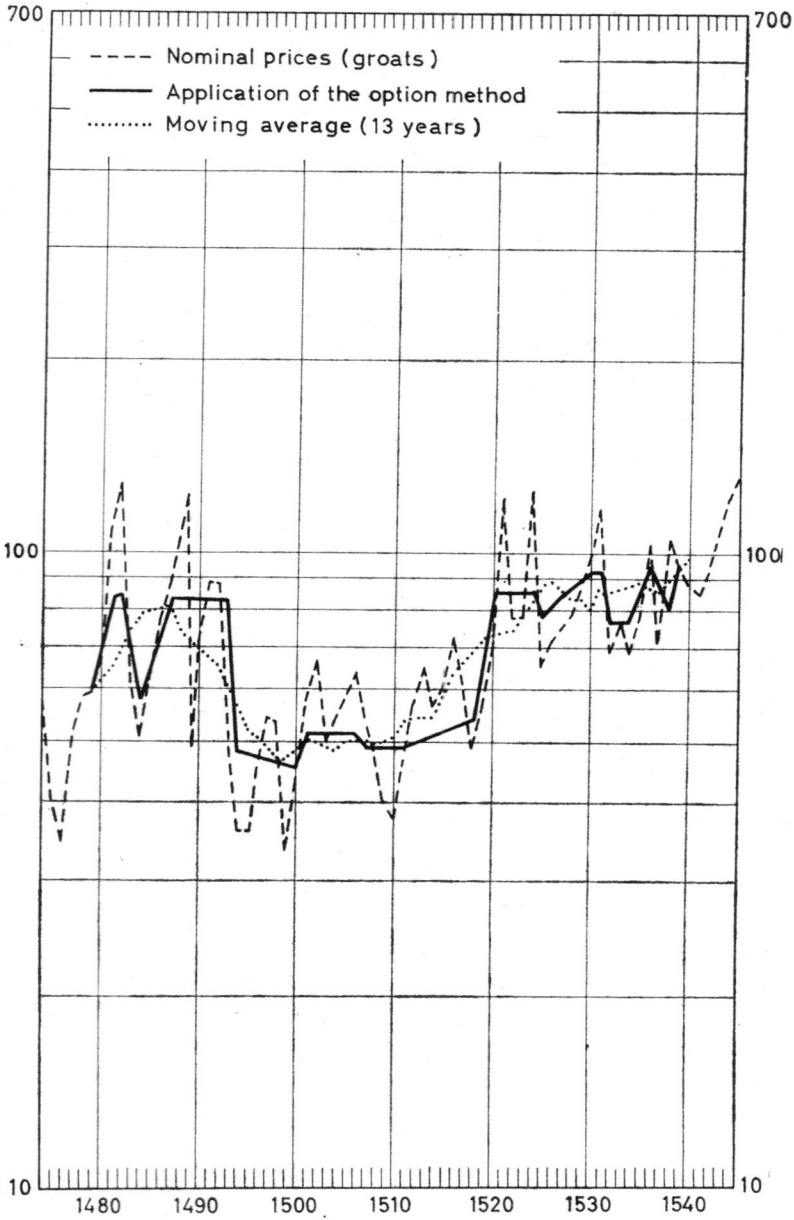

28

GRAPH 8

Comparison between methods of trend-calculation of wheat prices in Lier, in Brabant money of account (averages per harvest year).

GRAPH 9

Correlation between wheat prices of Lier, Flanders (see Van Houtte, *Prix*) and New Castile (see Hamilton, *Price revolution in Spain*) (1474-1545).

GRAPH 9

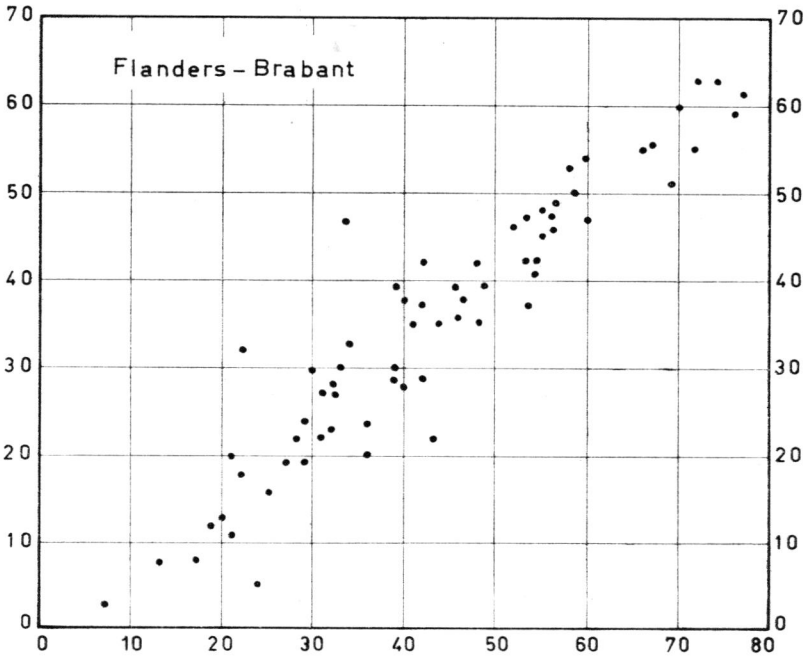

Flanders - Brabant

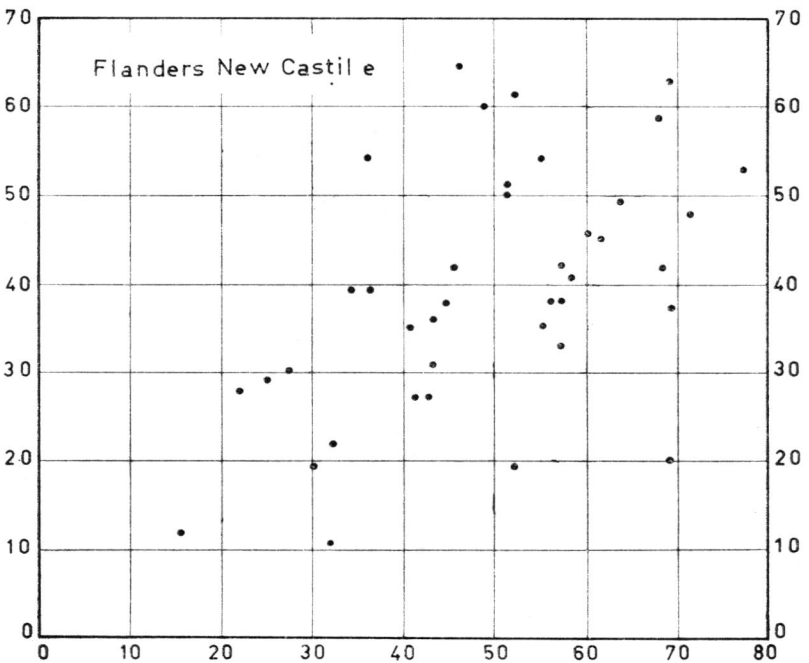

Flanders New Castile

GRAPH 10

Frequency curve for summer day wages (in Brabant groats) of masons in Antwerp from different sources (comparison with the modal average of wage-data of the Church of Our Lady) (1456-1600).

GRAPH 11

Seignorial farms, property of the Poor Relief of Lier (circa 1560).
Principal farms, property of Antwerp's St. Elisabeth's Hospital (circa 1560)

34

GRAPH 11

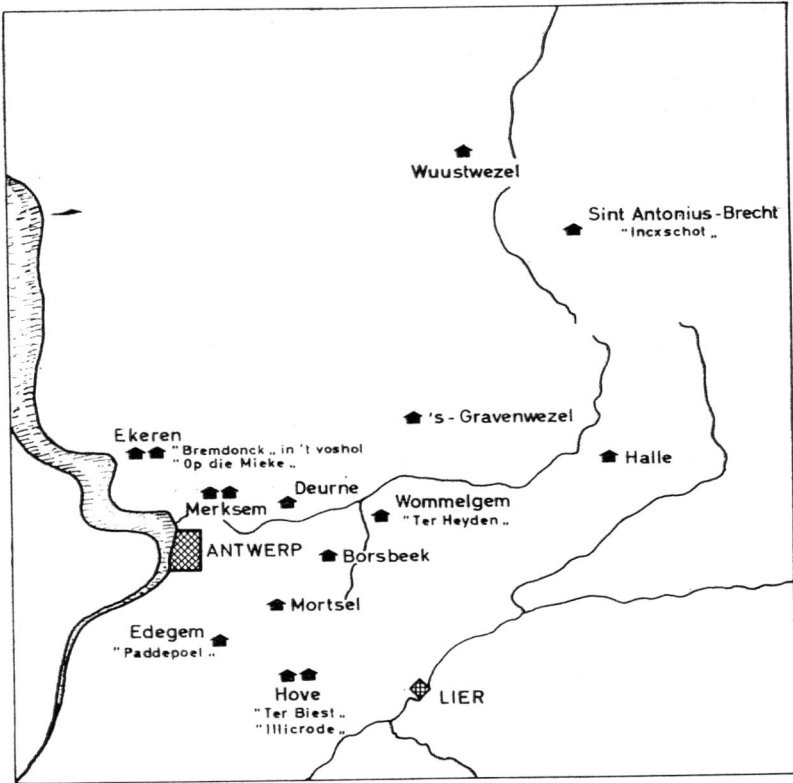

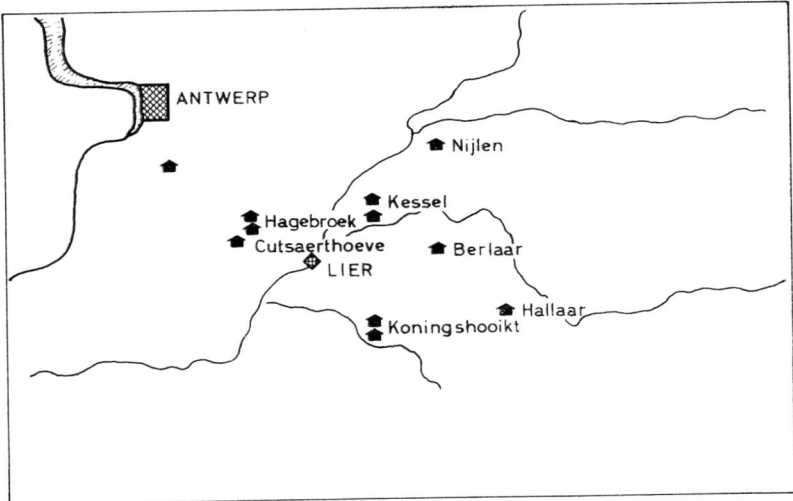

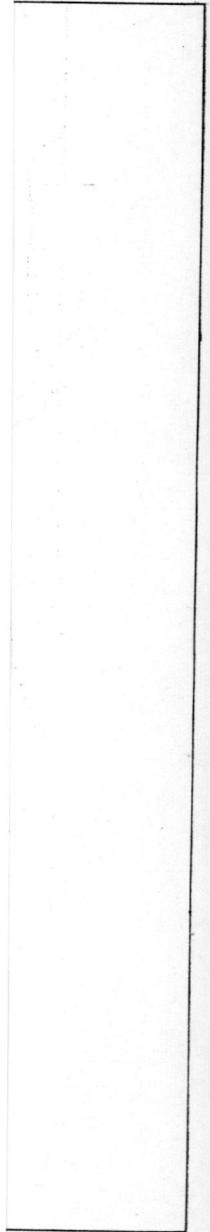

GRAPH 12

Farms, property of the Abbey of Tongerlo, or from which it had right to *métayage* on cattle (fifteenth century).

GRAPH 13

Nominal rye prices in Antwerp and nominal wages in Brabant : 1385-1439 (in Brabant money of account)

Rye : per Antwerp *viertel*
Mason and mason's labourer : per summer day
Linen weaver : per ell

Evolution of the real weight of fine silver in the Brabant groat : 1385-1409.

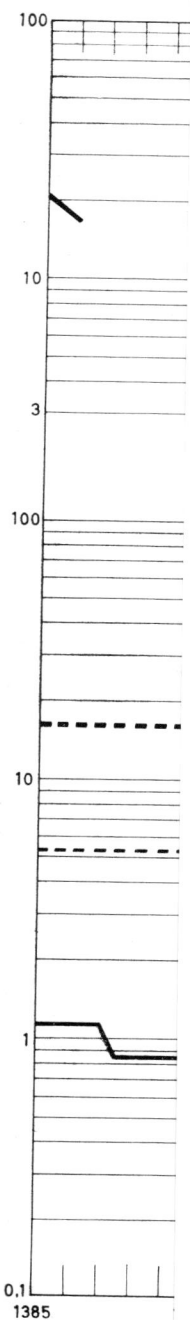

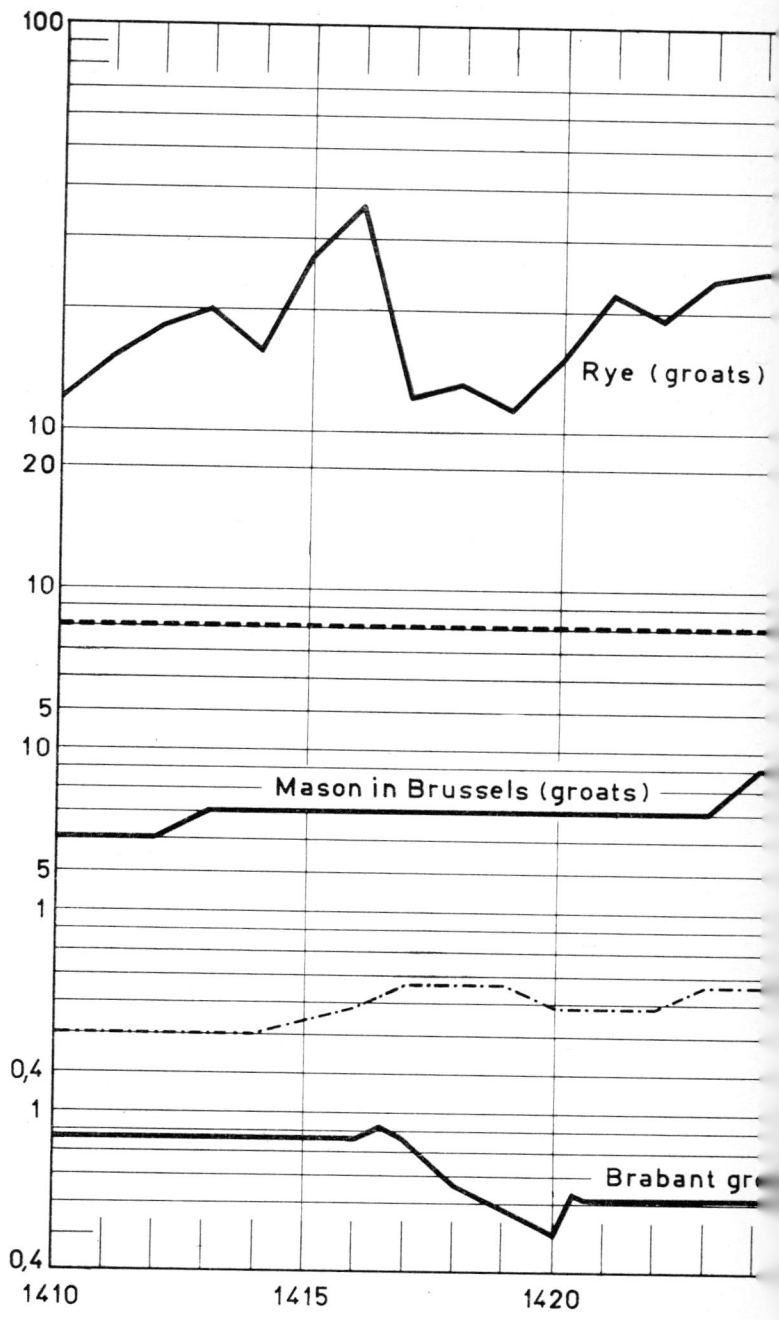

Rye (groats)

Mason in Brussels (groats)

Brabant gr

100

10

3

100

10

1

0,1
1385

100

20

10

5

10

5

1

0,4

1

0,4

1410

1415

1420

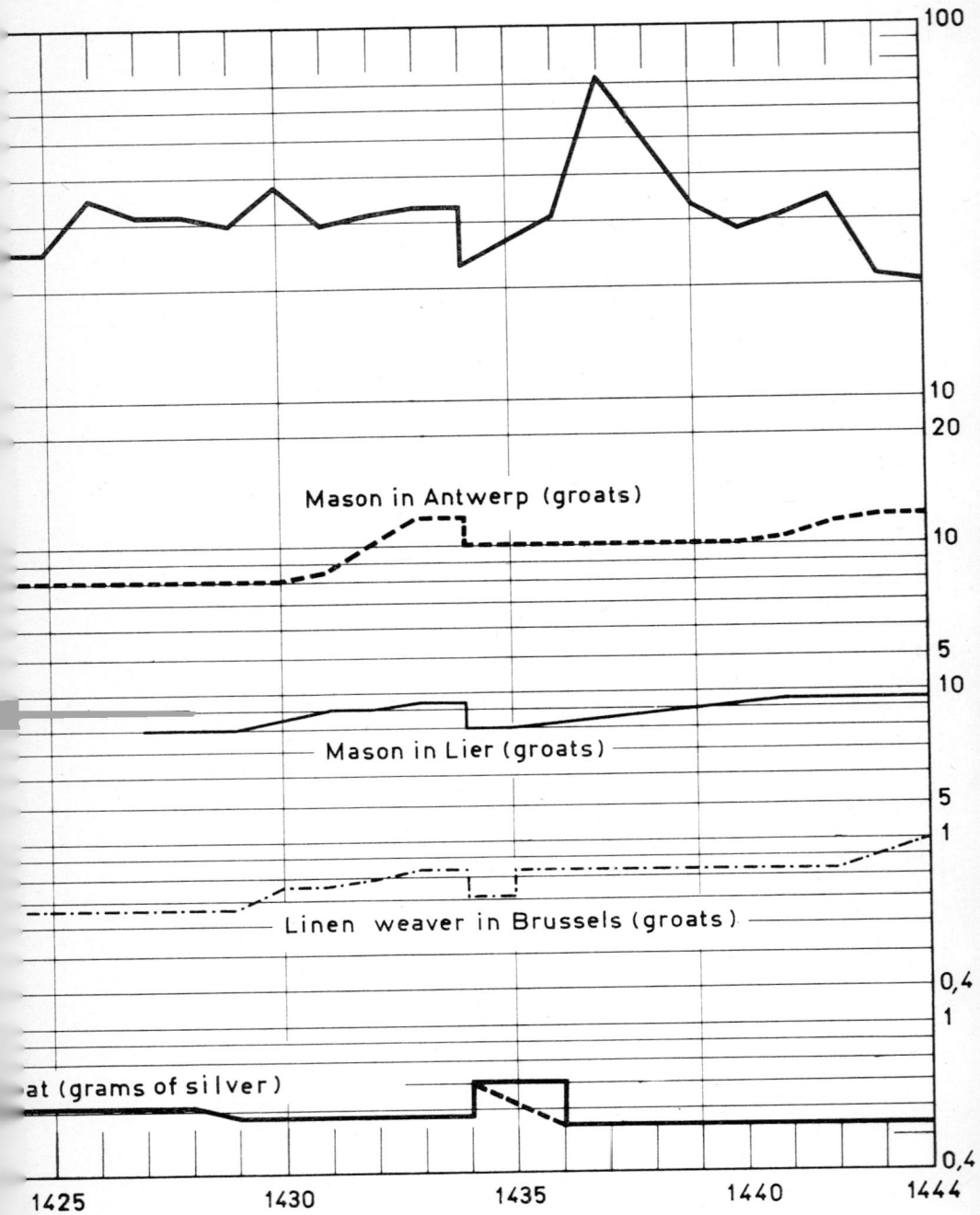

GRAPH 14

Mason in Antwerp (groats)

Mason in Lier (groats)

Linen weaver in Brussels (groats)

...at (grams of silver)

1425   1430   1435   1440   1444

GRAPH 14

Nominal rye prices in Antwerp and nominal wages in Brabant : 1410-1444 (in Brabant money of account).

Rye : per Antwerp *viertel*
Mason : per summer day
Linen weaver : per ell

Evolution of the official and real weight of fine silver in the Brabant groat : 1410-1444.

GRAPH 15

Nominal prices and wages in Brabant : 1430-1480 (in Brabant money of account).

Herring : per *ton*
Cheese : per *wage*
Rye : per Antwerp *viertel*
Flax : per *steen*
Cloth : per ell of Antwerp
Rhine wine : per *gelte* of Lier
Salt : per *vat*
Mason : per summer day
Pepper and sugar : per pound of Antwerp
Linen weaver : per ell of Brussels

GRAPH 16

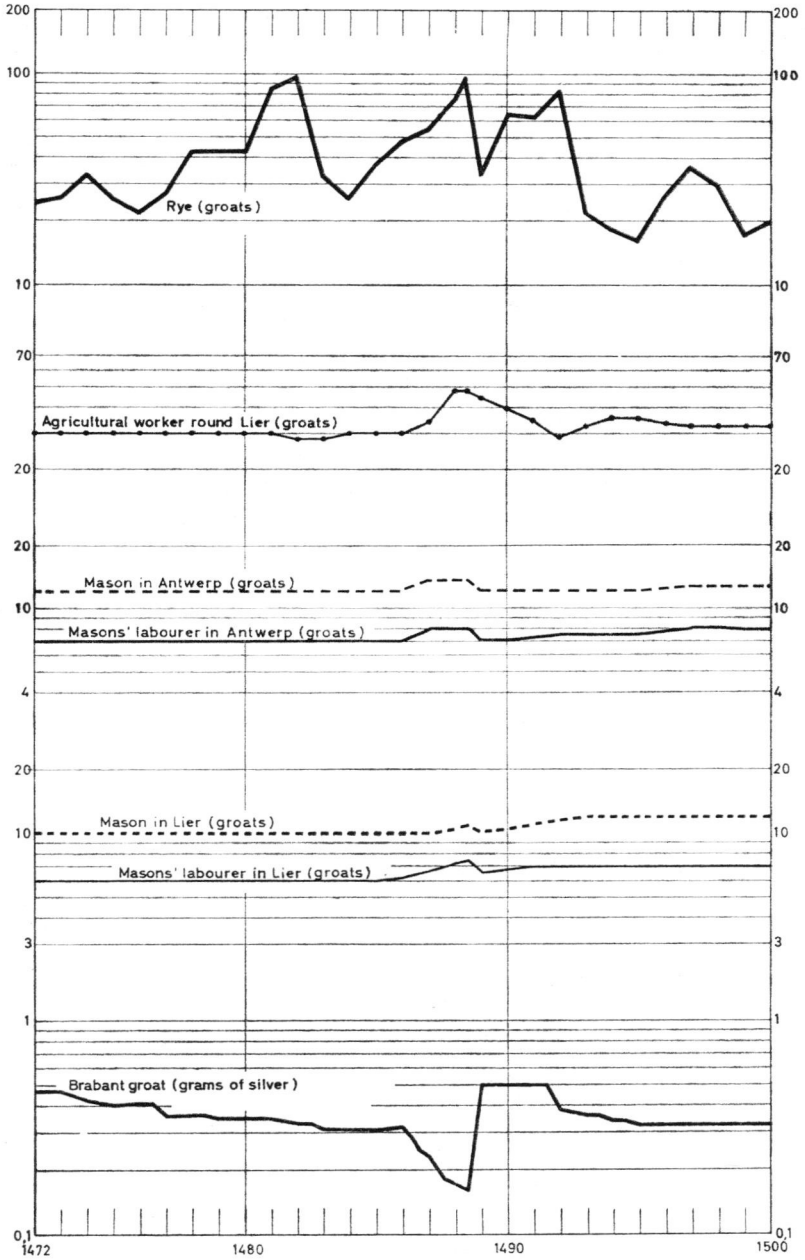

Rye (groats)

Agricultural worker round Lier (groats)

Mason in Antwerp (groats)

Masons' labourer in Antwerp (groats)

Mason in Lier (groats)

Masons' labourer in Lier (groats)

Brabant groat (grams of silver)

44

GRAPH 15

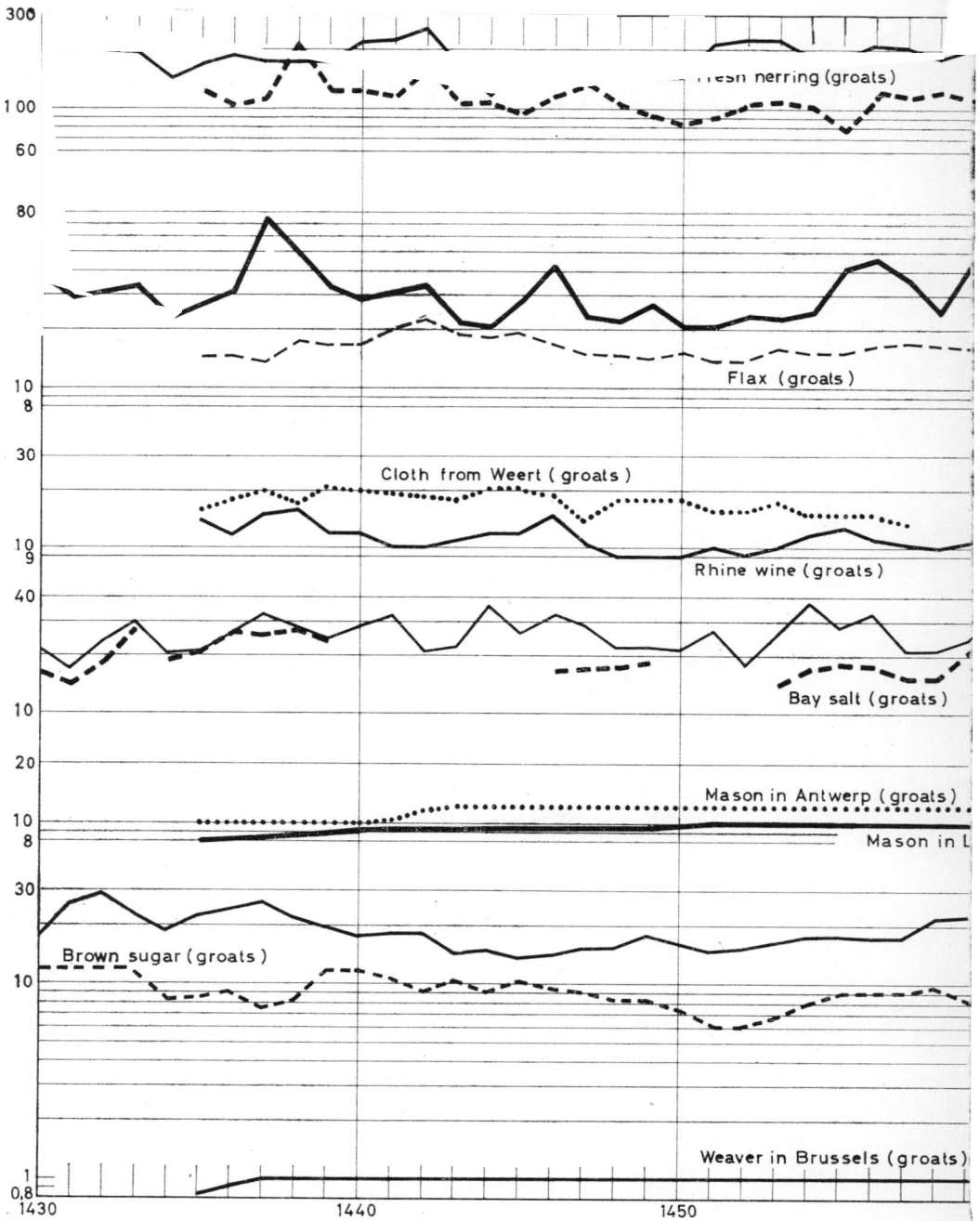

Fresh herring (groats)

Flax (groats)

Cloth from Weert (groats)

Rhine wine (groats)

Bay salt (groats)

Mason in Antwerp (groats)

Mason in L

Brown sugar (groats)

Weaver in Brussels (groats)

GRAPH 16

Nominal prices and wages in Brabant : 1472-1500 (in Brabant money of account).

Rye : per Antwerp *viertel*
Agricultural worker : per 1000 fagots
Mason and mason's labourer : per summer day

Evolution of the official and real weight of fine silver in the Brabant groat : 1472-1500.

GRAPH 17

Nominal prices and wages in Brabant : 1489-1525 (in Brabant money of account).

Rye : per Antwerp *viertel*
Butter and meat : per 100 pounds
Mason and mason's labourer : per summer day
Agricultural worker : per 1000 fagots
Bricks : per 1000 pieces
Cloth : per ell of Antwerp
Lime : per *viertel* of Lier
Pepper and sugar : per pound of Antwerp
Linen weaver : per ell of Brussels

GRAPH 17

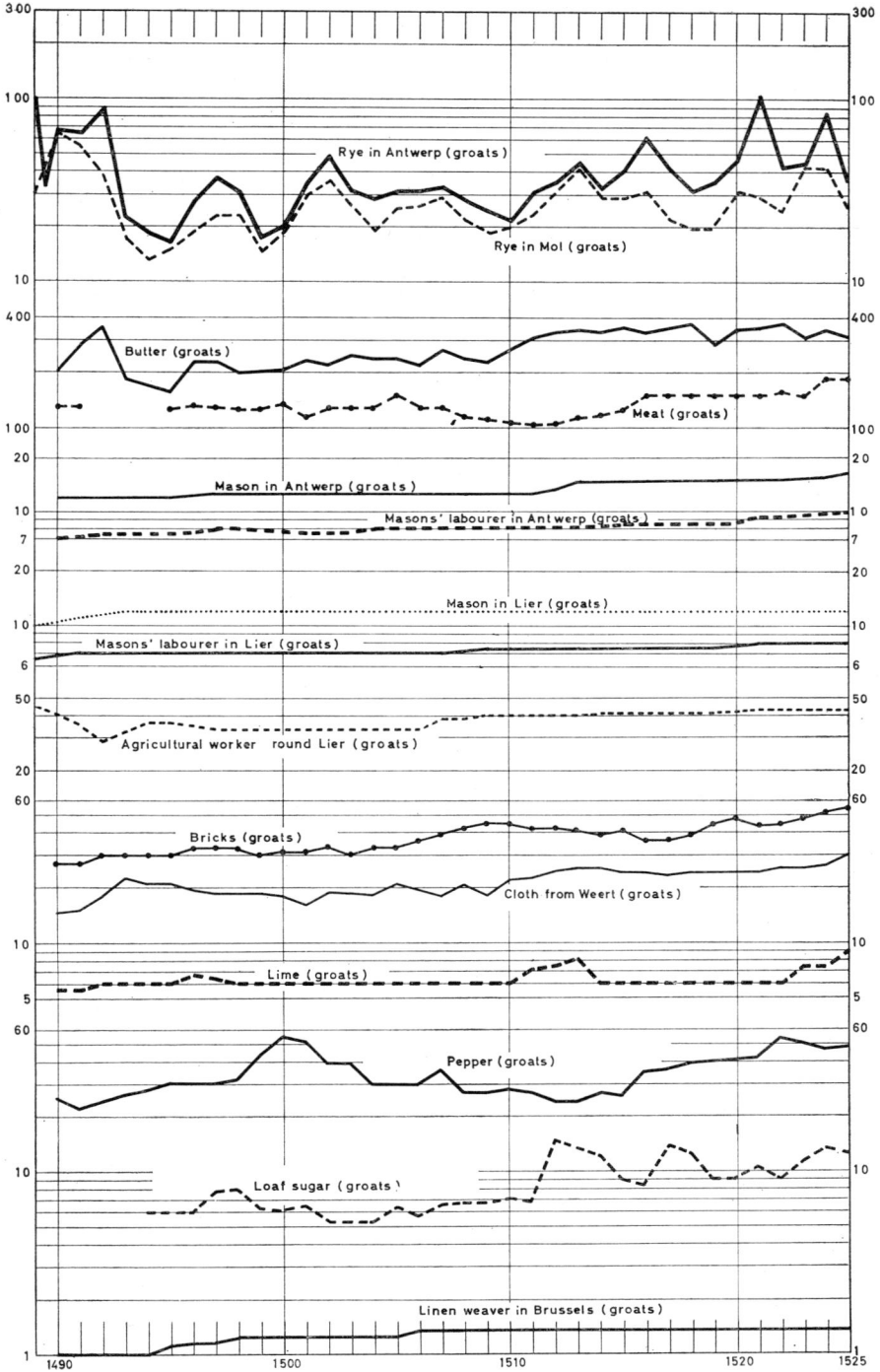

Rye in Antwerp (groats)

Rye in Mol (groats)

Butter (groats)

Meat (groats)

Mason in Antwerp (groats)

Masons' labourer in Antwerp (groats)

Mason in Lier (groats)

Masons' labourer in Lier (groats)

Agricultural worker round Lier (groats)

Bricks (groats)

Cloth from Weert (groats)

Lime (groats)

Pepper (groats)

Loaf sugar (groats)

Linen weaver in Brussels (groats)

47

GRAPH 18

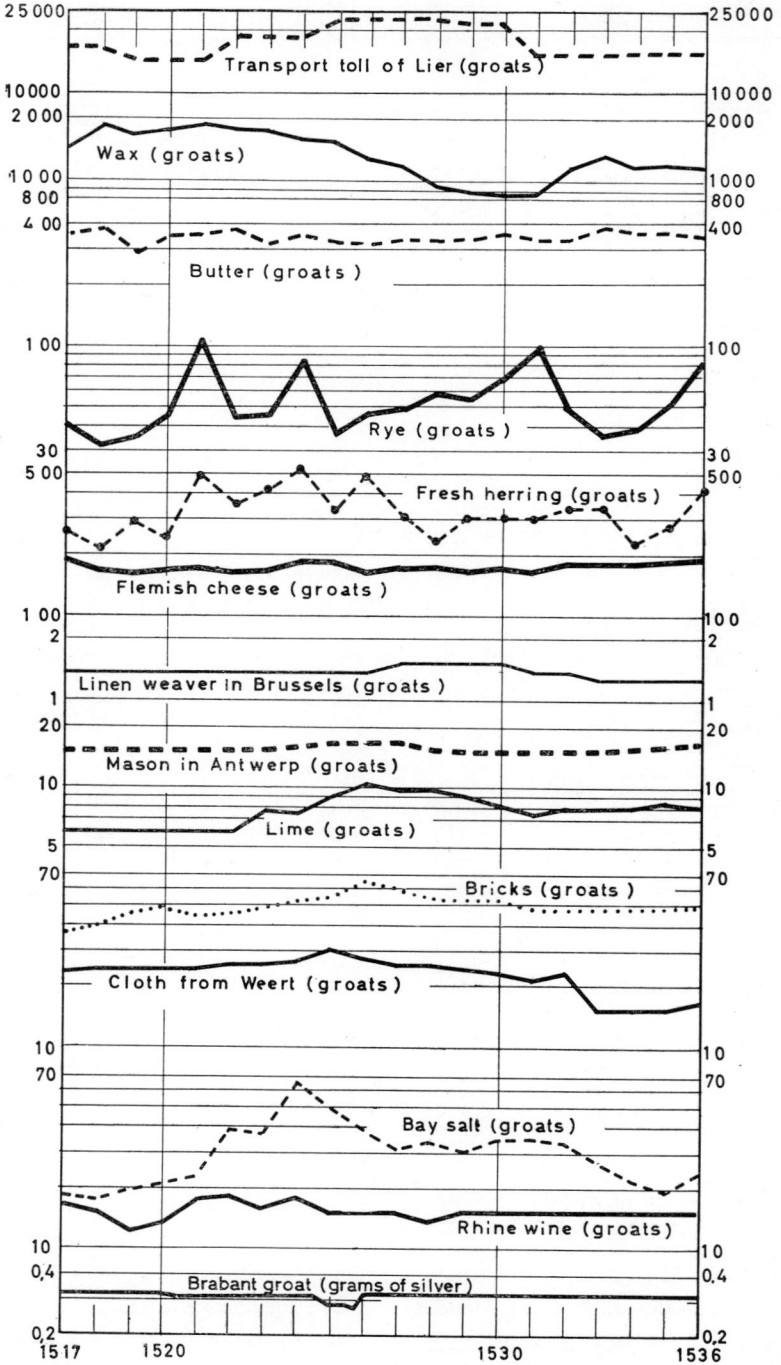

Transport toll of Lier (groats)

Wax (groats)

Butter (groats)

Rye (groats)

Fresh herring (groats)

Flemish cheese (groats)

Linen weaver in Brussels (groats)

Mason in Antwerp (groats)

Lime (groats)

Bricks (groats)

Cloth from Weert (groats)

Bay salt (groats)

Rhine wine (groats)

Brabant groat (grams of silver)

GRAPH 18

Nominal prices, wages and other statistics in Brabant: 1517-1536 (in Brabant money of account).

Wax and butter : per 100 pounds
Rye : per Antwerp *viertel*
Herring : per *vat*
Cheese : per *wage*
Linen weaver : per ell of Brussels
Mason : per summer day
Lime : per *viertel* of Lier
Bricks : per 1000 pieces
Cloth : per ell of Antwerp
Salt : per *vat*
Wine : per *gelte* of Lier.

Evolution of the official weight of fine silver in the Brabant groat : 1517-1536.

Nominal prices in Brabant : 1515-1555 (in Brabant money of account).

Rye : per Antwerp *viertel*
Sail-cloth : per Antwerp ell

GRAPH 19

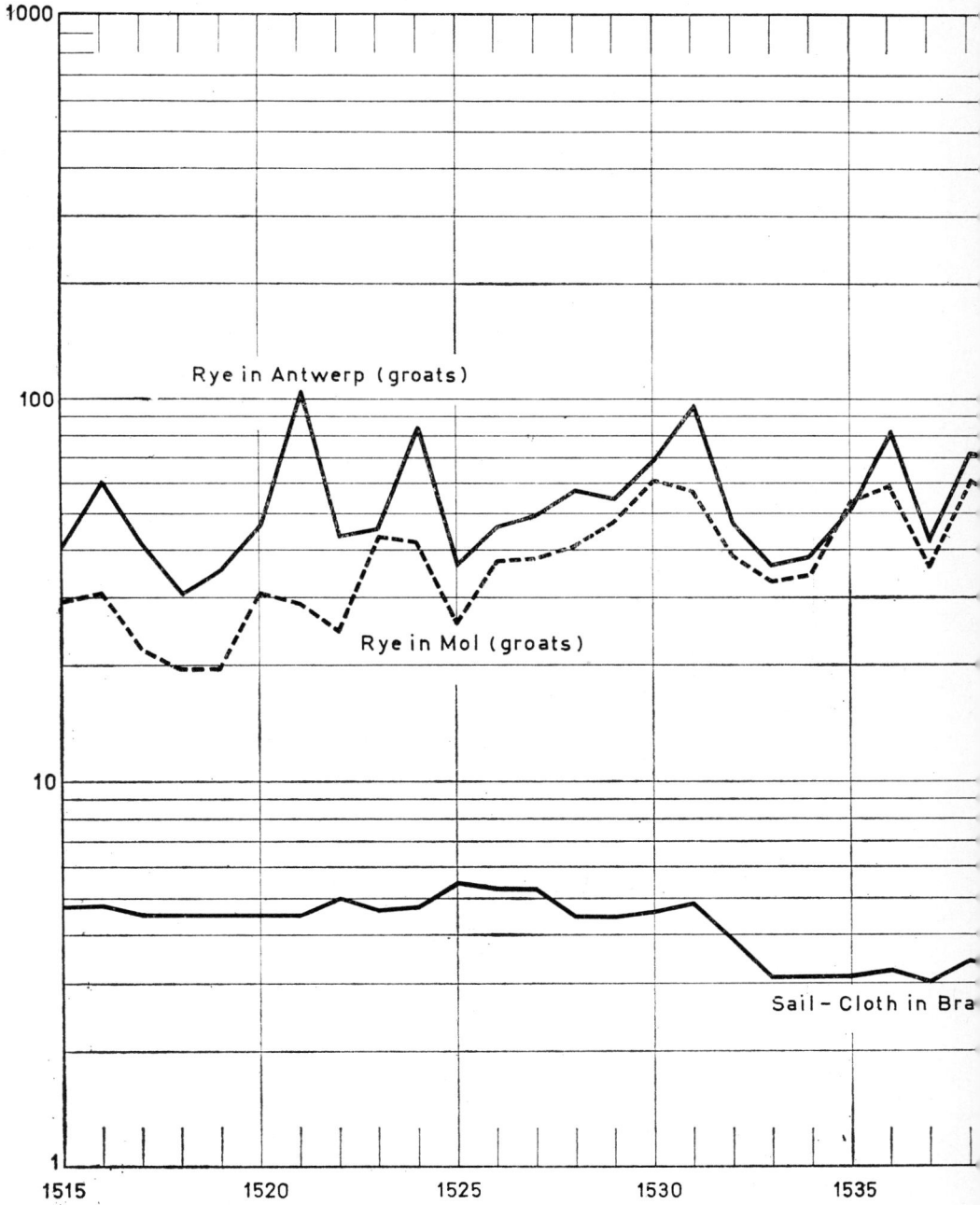

Rye in Antwerp (groats)

Rye in Mol (groats)

Sail – Cloth in Bra

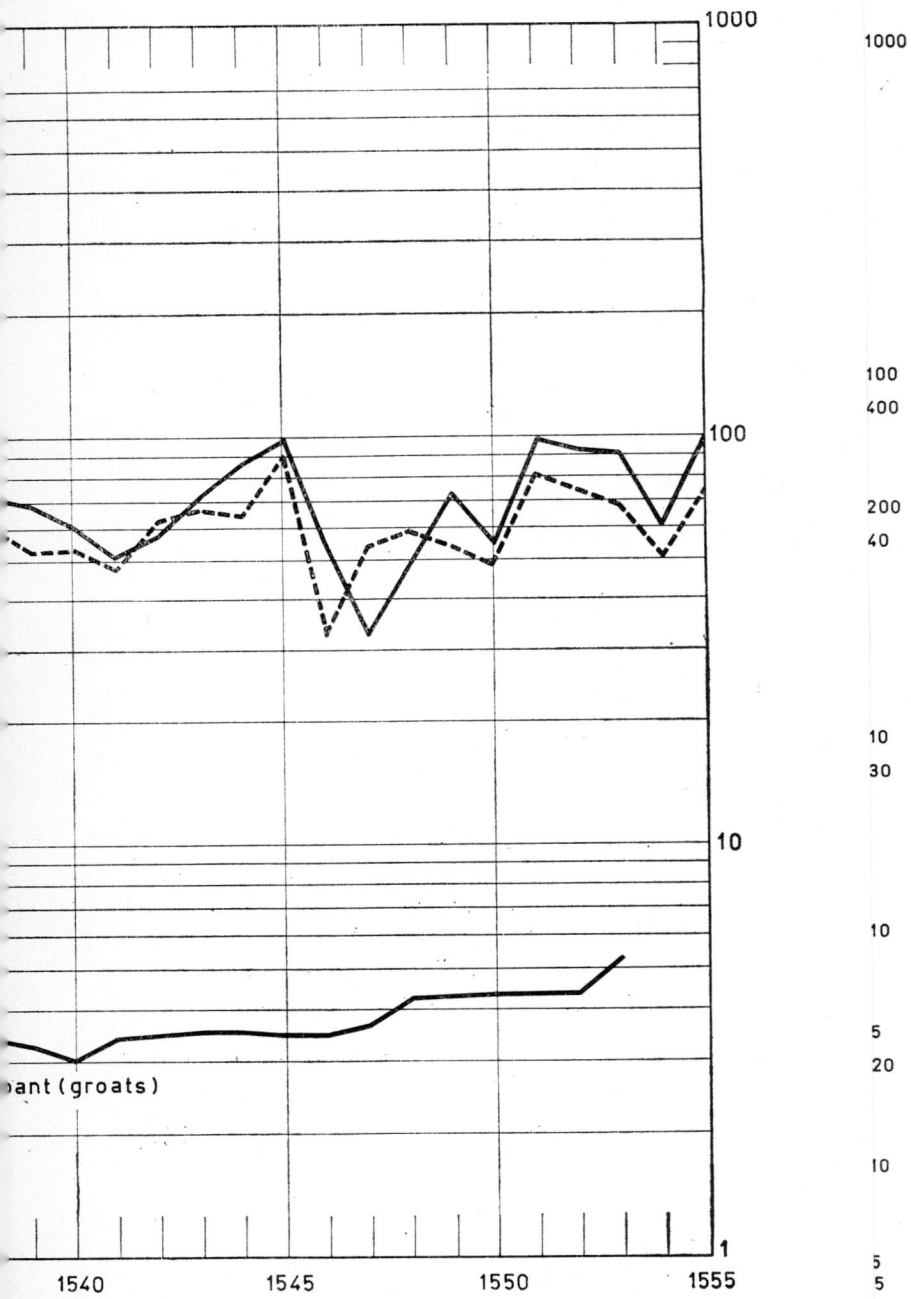

ant (groats)

1000
1000

100
400

100

200

40

10
30

10

10

5
20

10

5
5

1540   1545   1550   1555

GRAPH 20

Nominal prices and wages in Brabant : 1535-1555 (in Brabant money of account).

Butter and meat : per 100 pounds
Cheese : per *wage*
Cloth : per Antwerp ell
Mason and mason's labourer : per summer day

53

GRAPH 21

Nominal prices and wages in Brabant : 1553-1573 (in Brabant money of account).

Butter and meat : per 100 pounds
Cheese : per *wage*
Rye : per Antwerp *viertel*
Bricks : per 1000 pieces
Cloth : per Antwerp ell
Lime : per Lier *viertel*
Agricultural worker : per 1000 fagots
Mason and mason's labourer : per summer day

Evolution of the official weight of fine silver in the Brabant groat: 1553-1573.

GRAPH 21

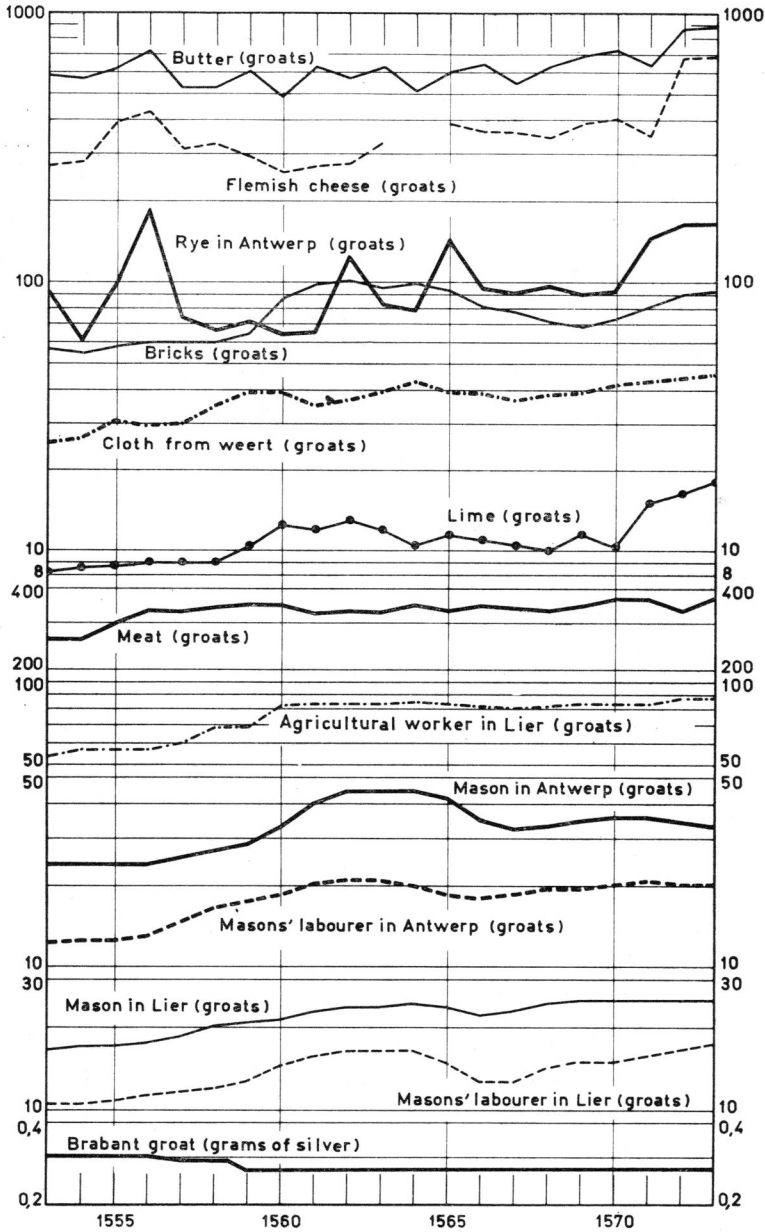

Butter (groats)

Flemish cheese (groats)

Rye in Antwerp (groats)

Bricks (groats)

Cloth from weert (groats)

Lime (groats)

Meat (groats)

Agricultural worker in Lier (groats)

Mason in Antwerp (groats)

Masons' labourer in Antwerp (groats)

Mason in Lier (groats)

Masons' labourer in Lier (groats)

Brabant groat (grams of silver)

55

GRAPH 22

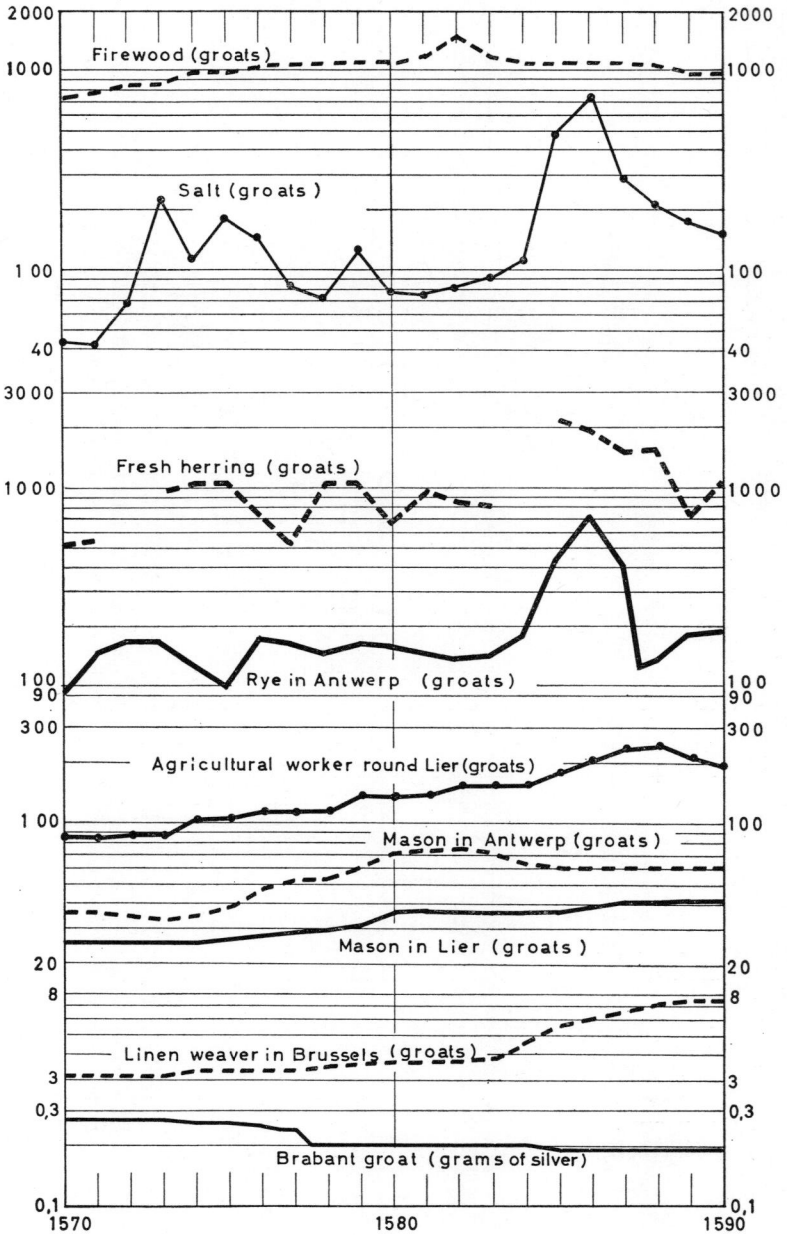

Firewood (groats)

Salt (groats)

Fresh herring (groats)

Rye in Antwerp (groats)

Agricultural worker round Lier(groats)

Mason in Antwerp (groats)

Mason in Lier (groats)

Linen weaver in Brussels (groats)

Brabant groat (grams of silver)

GRAPH 22

Nominal prices and wages in Brabant : 1570-1590 (in Brabant money of account).

Firewood : per 1000 fagots
Salt and herring : per *vat*
Rye : per Antwerp *viertel*
Agricultural worker : per 1000 fagots
Mason : per summer day
Linen weaver : per ell of Brussels

Evolution of the official weight of fine silver in the Brabant groat : 1570-1590.

GRAPH 23

Nominal prices and wages in Brabant : 1581-1600 (in Brabant money of account).

Rye : per Antwerp *viertel*
Agricultural worker : per 1000 fagots
Mason : per summer day
Cloth : per Antwerp ell
Lime : per *viertel* of Lier

58

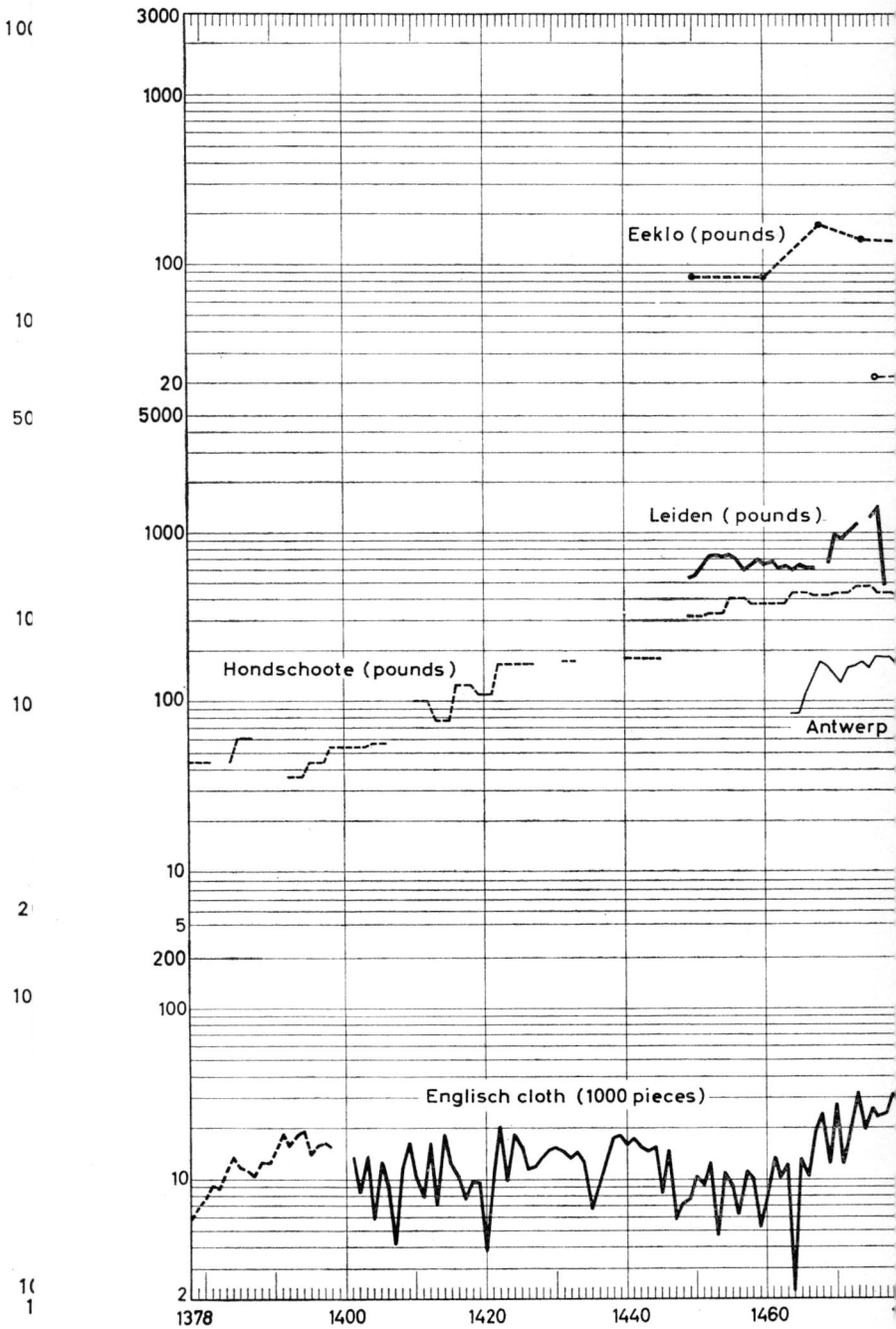

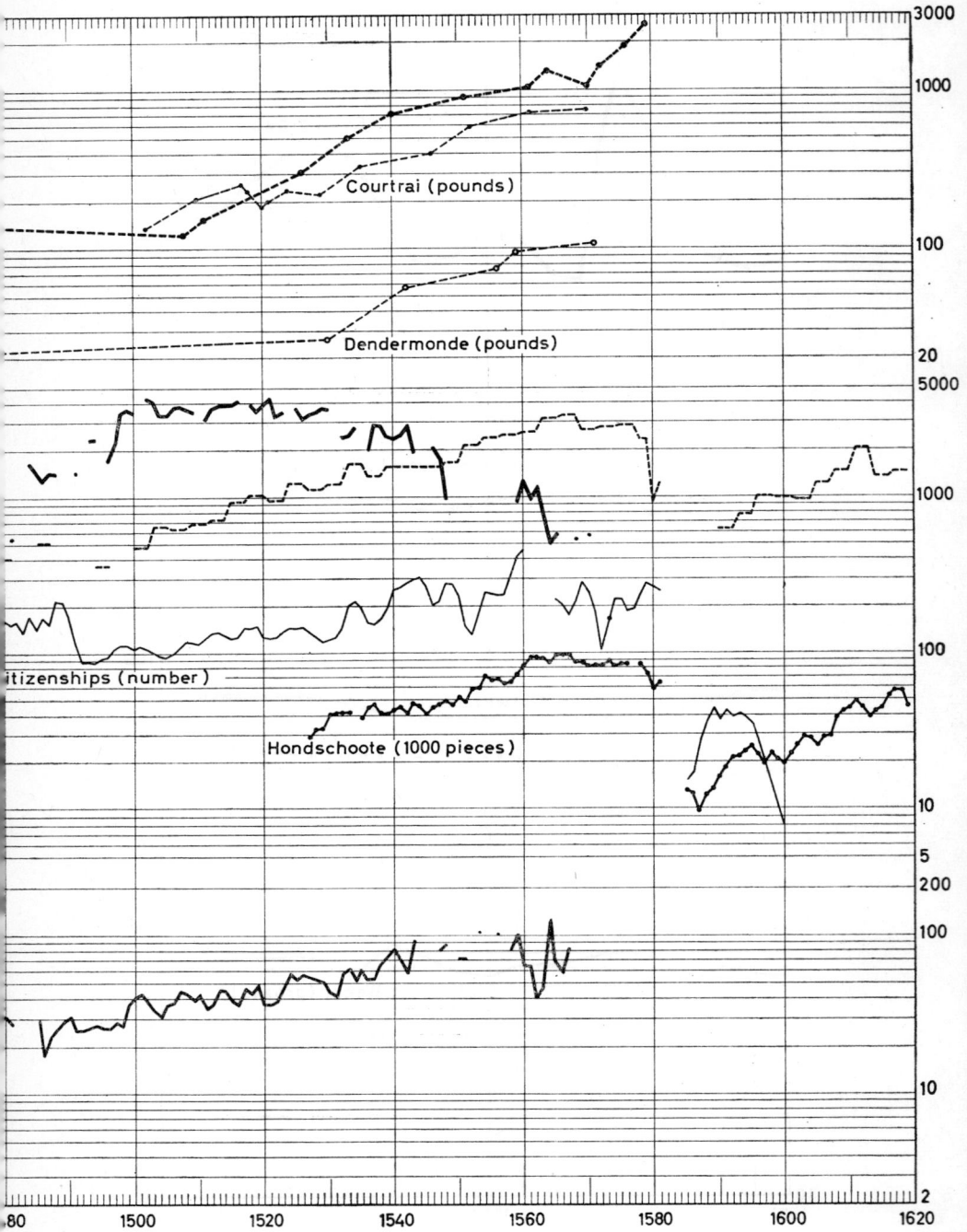

GRAPH 24

Courtrai (pounds)

Dendermonde (pounds)

itizenships (number)

Hondschoote (1000 pieces)

GRAPH 24

Statistics of production, commerce and immigration : 1378-1620.

1 Flemish linen : from linen excise income in Courtrai, Eeklo and Dendermonde (see SABBE, *Belgische vlasnijverheid*, I).

2 Cloth of Leiden : from the *strykerye* income (see POSTHUMUS, *Leidsche lakenindustrie*).

3 Says of Hondschoote : from the count's income from the farm (in pounds) and from the export figures (per 1000 pieces) (see COORNAERT, *Hondschoote*).

4 Immigration : from the yearly number of Antwerp citizenships bought by immigrants (connected by three yearly moving averages).

5 Transit-trade of English cloth : from the annual export-figures of London (see CARUS-WILSON, POWER-POSTAN, RAMSEY, SCHANZ, FISHER).

61

GRAPH 25

Number of apprentices received yearly into the Weavers'guild of Brussels : 1417-1446.

GRAPH 25

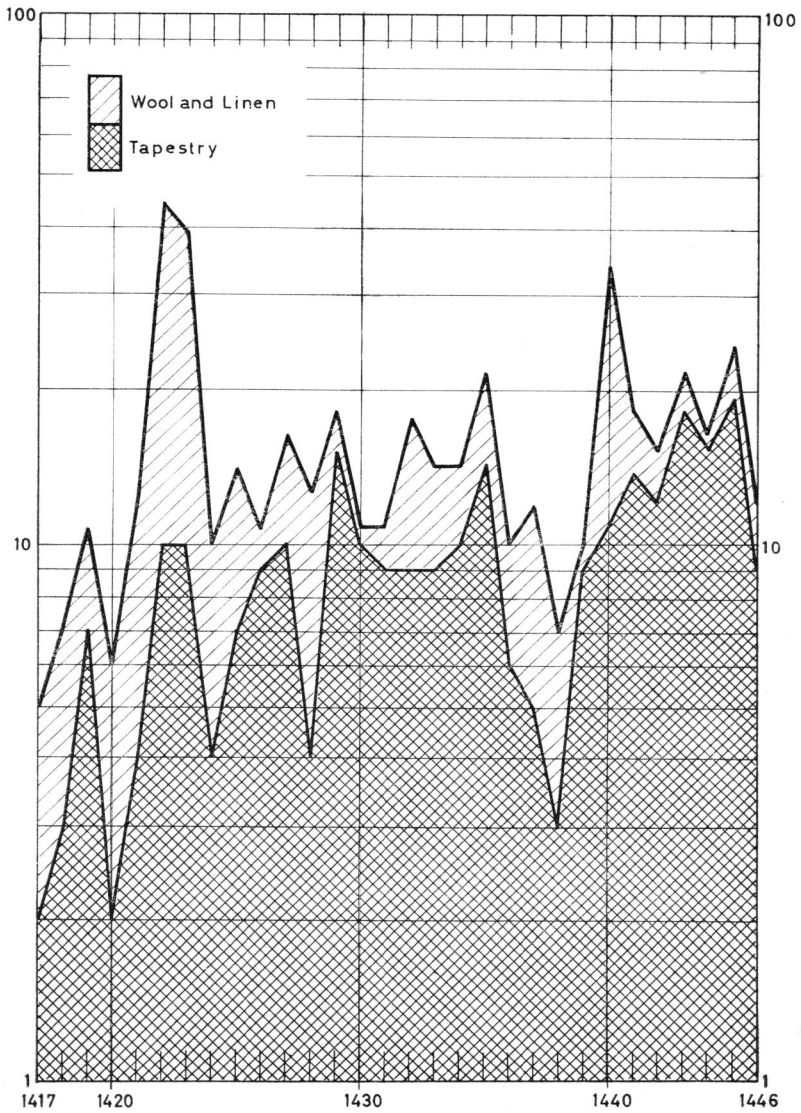

GRAPH 26

Annual income from excise of Bergen-op-Zoom : 1442-1555 (in pounds Artois).

GRAPH 27

Hungarian copper exported by the Fuggers : 1497-1539 (per 100 Antwerp pounds).

GRAPH 27

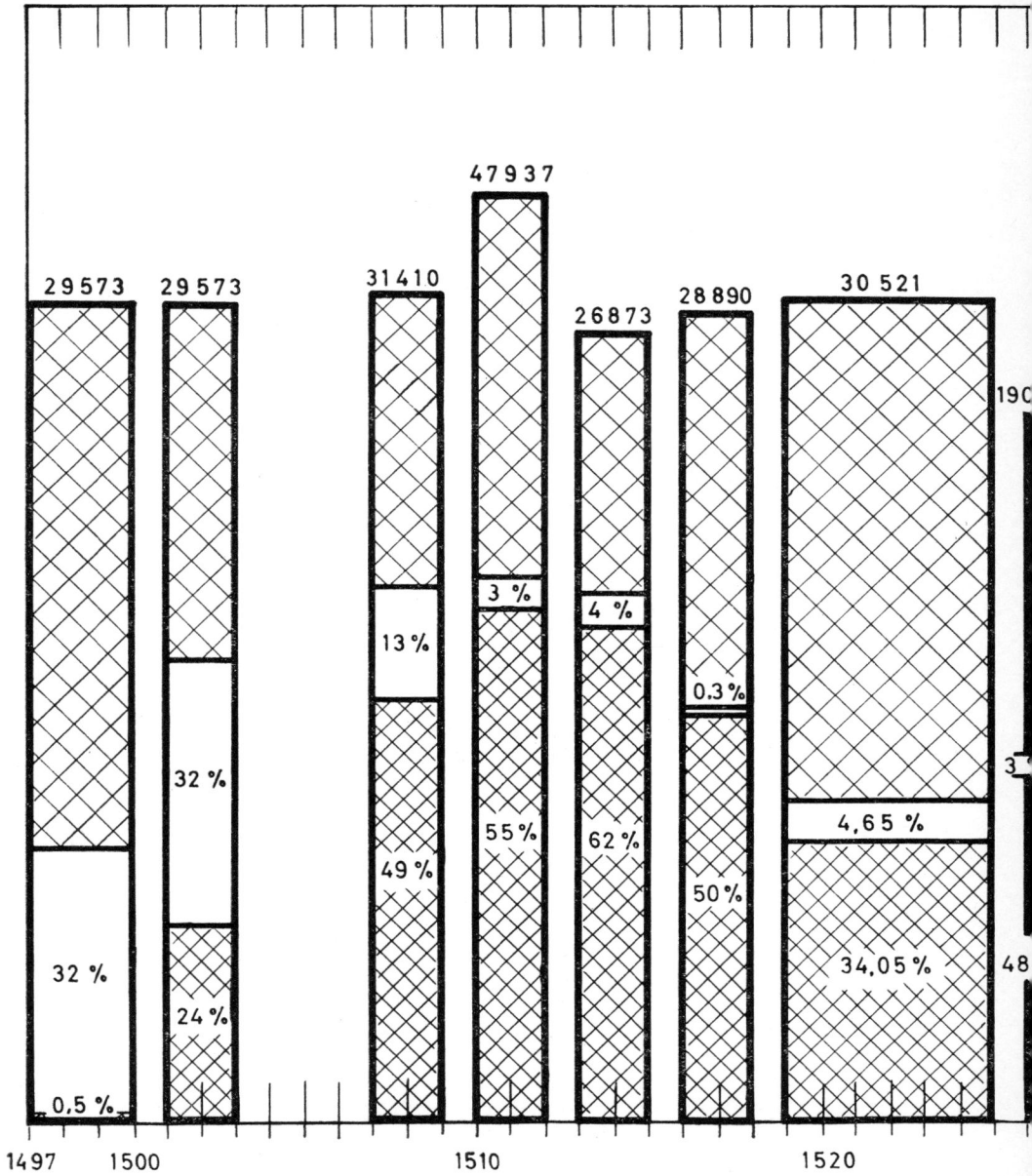

47937

29573   29573   31410   26873   28890   30521

190

3

13 %   3 %   4 %
                        0.3 %

32 %   49 %   55 %   62 %   4,65 %
                                        50 %
                                                  34,05 %   48

32 %
        24 %

0.5 %

1497   1500   1510   1520

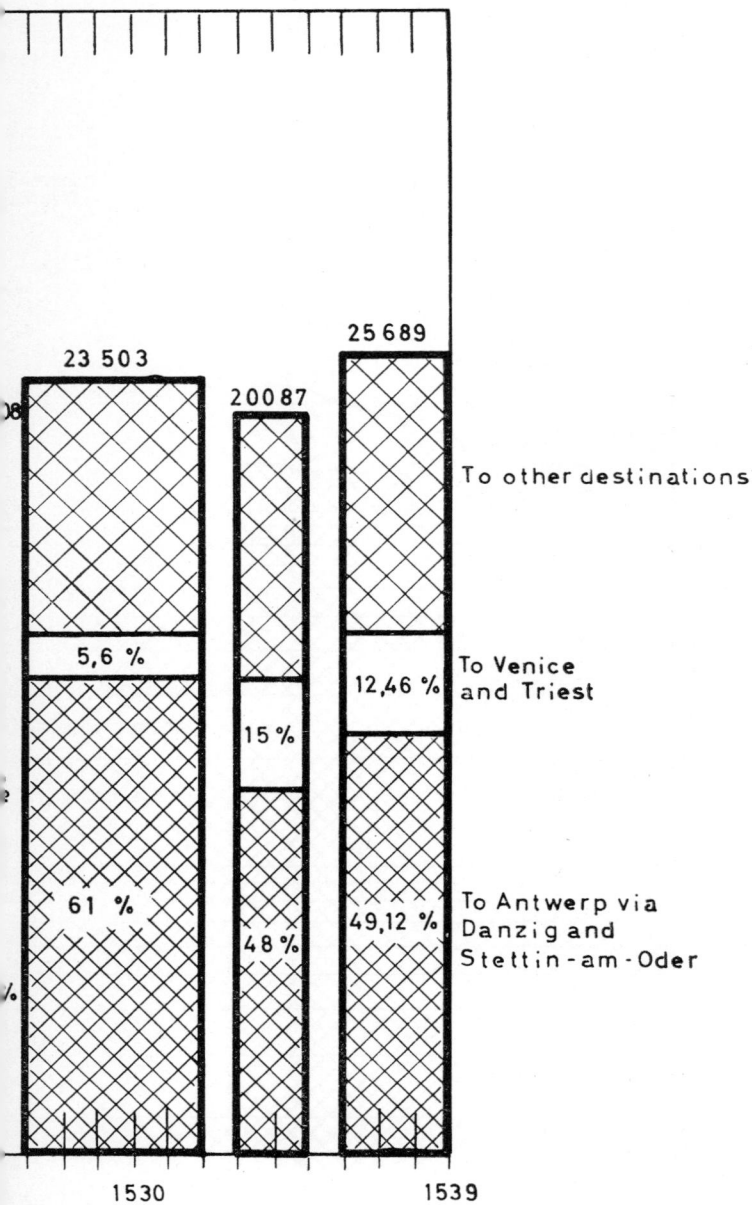

23 503

20 087

25 689

5,6 %

15 %

12,46 %

To other destinations

To Venice and Triest

61 %

48 %

49,12 %

To Antwerp via Danzig and Stettin-am-Oder

1530

1539

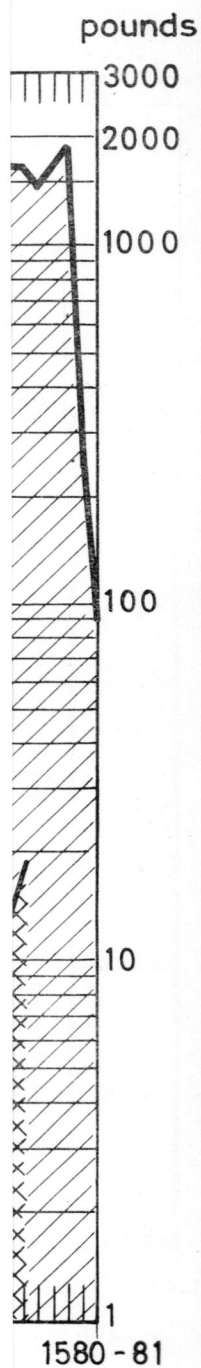

pounds

3000
2000
1000
100
10
1

1580 - 81

Annual income from rents of stalls (let during the Fairs only) and of shops (let during the whole year), belonging to the Church of Our Lady in Antwerp : 1470-1581 (in Brabant money of account).

GRAPH 29

Rents in and round Antwerp and Lier : 1440-1610.

1 Cloth hall : in Brabant money of account
2 Others : by indices (1568 = 100).

70

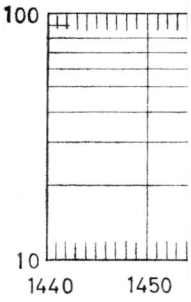

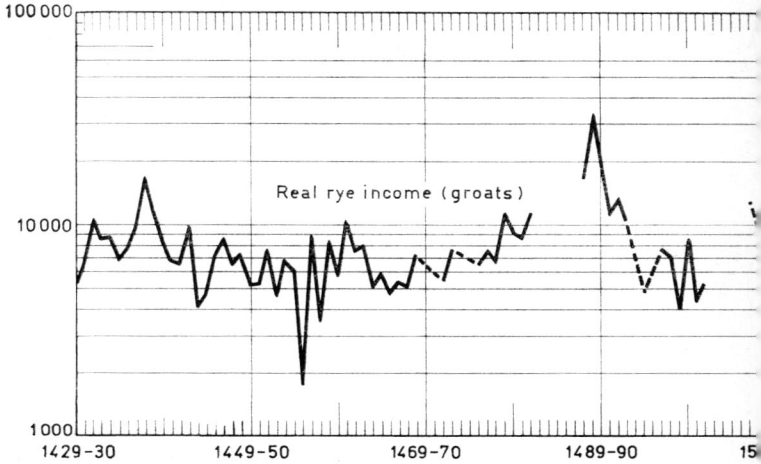

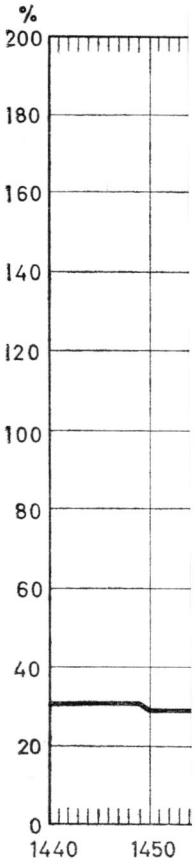

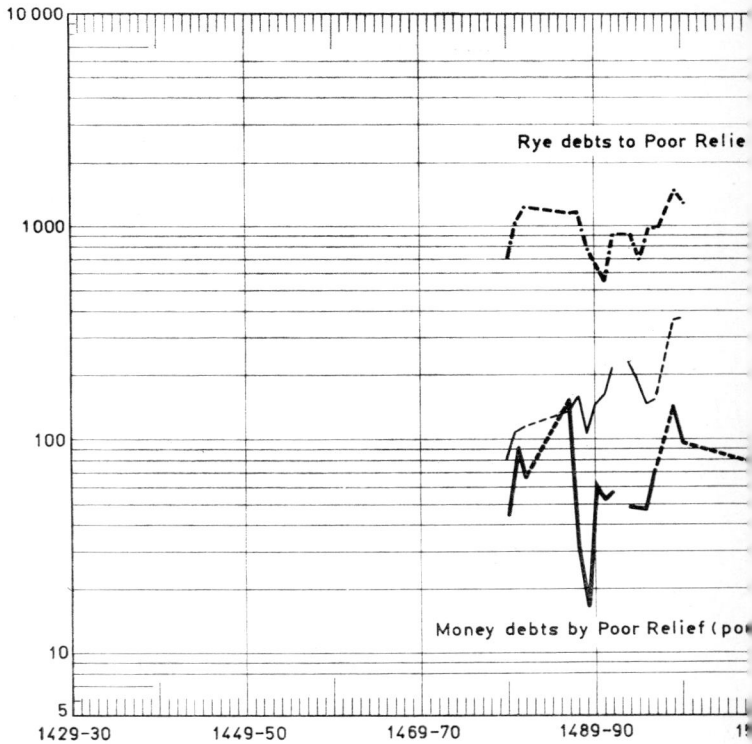

72

GRAPH 30

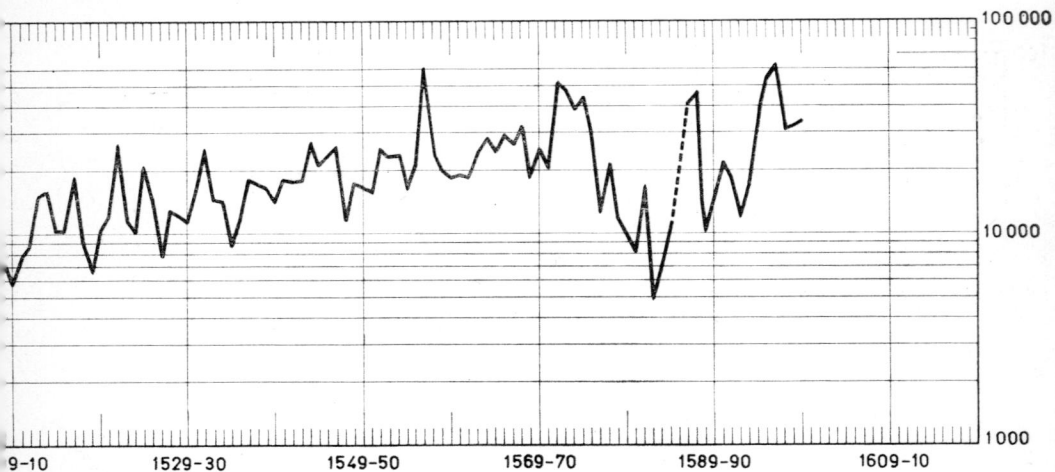

100 000

10 000

1 000

9–10   1529–30   1549–50   1569–70   1589–90   1609–10

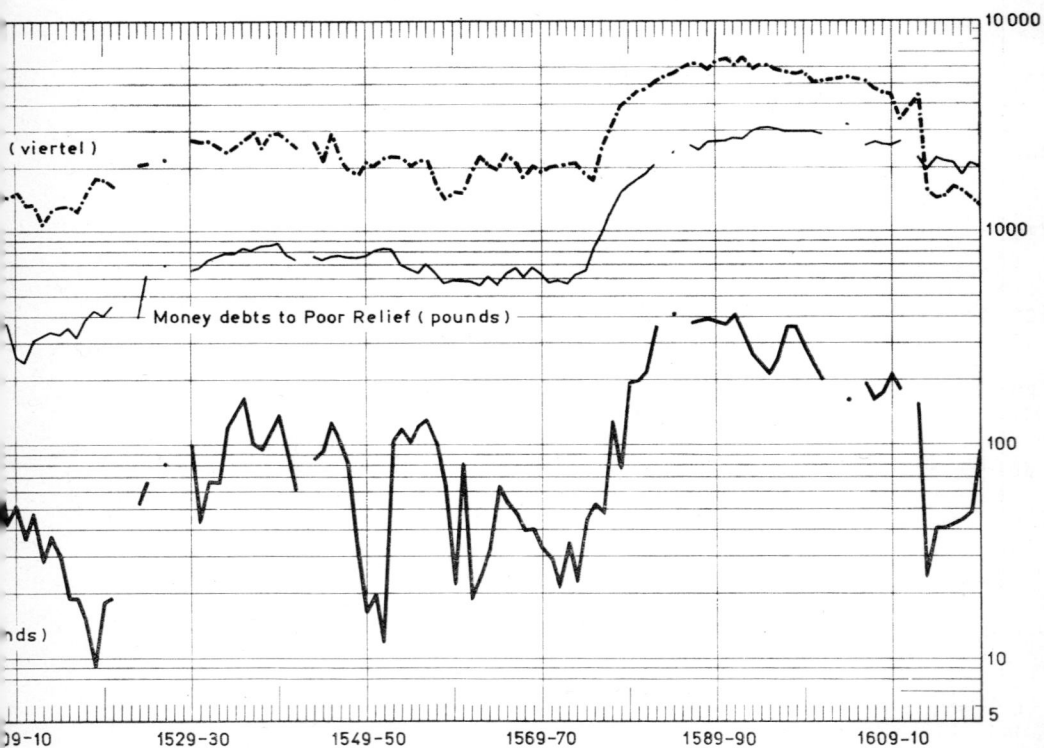

10 000

(viertel)

Money debts to Poor Relief (pounds)

1000

100

nds)

10

5

09–10   1529–30   1549–50   1569–70   1589–90   1609–10

GRAPH 30

Agricultural income in Brabant : 1429-1620.

1 Value of the annual *real* rye income of the Poor Relief of Lier from five
farms : 1429-1600 (in Brabant money of account).

2 Annual debit and credit balances of the Poor Relief of Lier : 1480-1620
(per Lier *viertel* or in Brabant money of account).

GRAPH 31

Annual comparison between *real* rye income of the Poor Relief of Lier and that *due* to it from the farmers (the amount due = 100) (1480-1600).

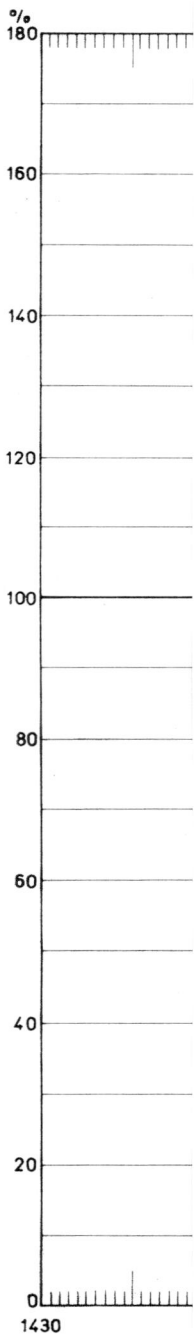

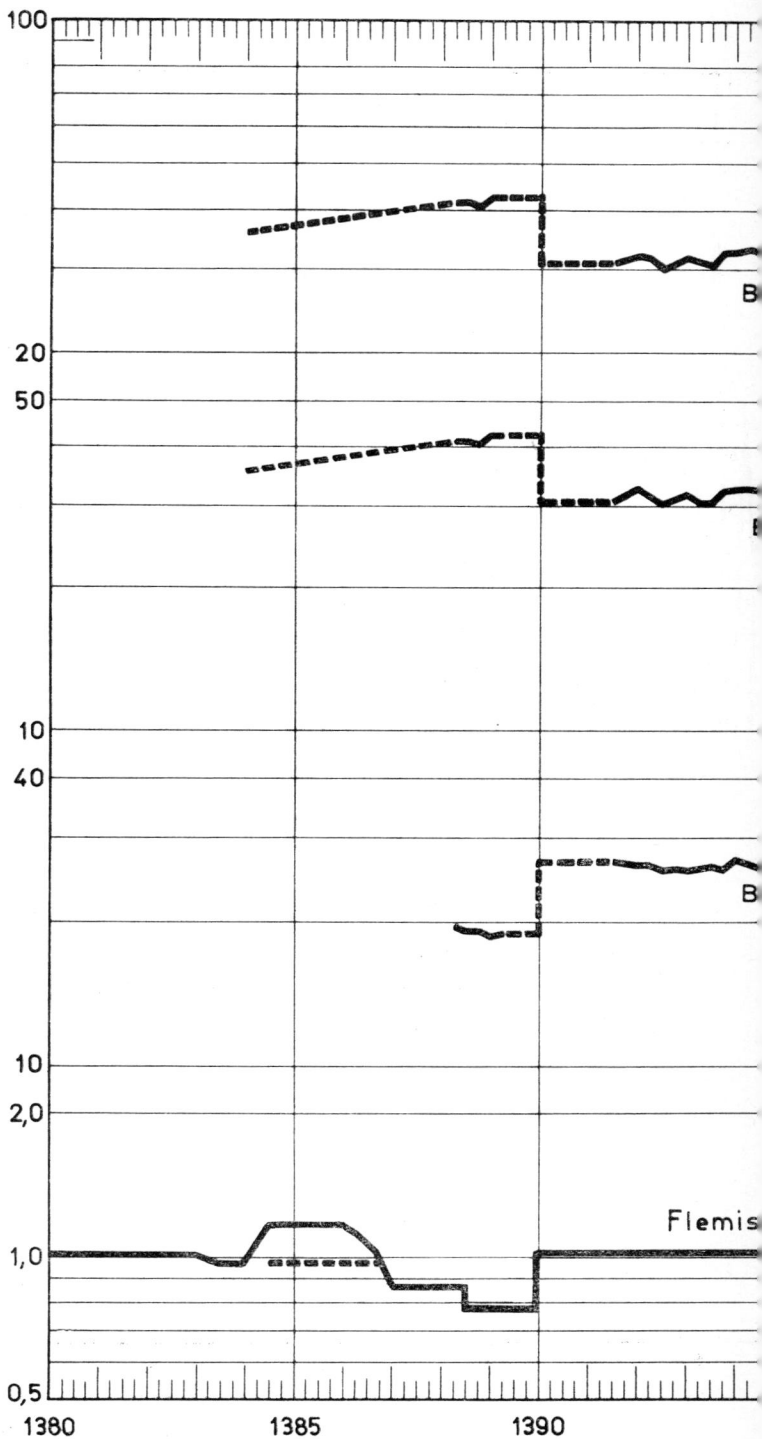

GRAPH 32

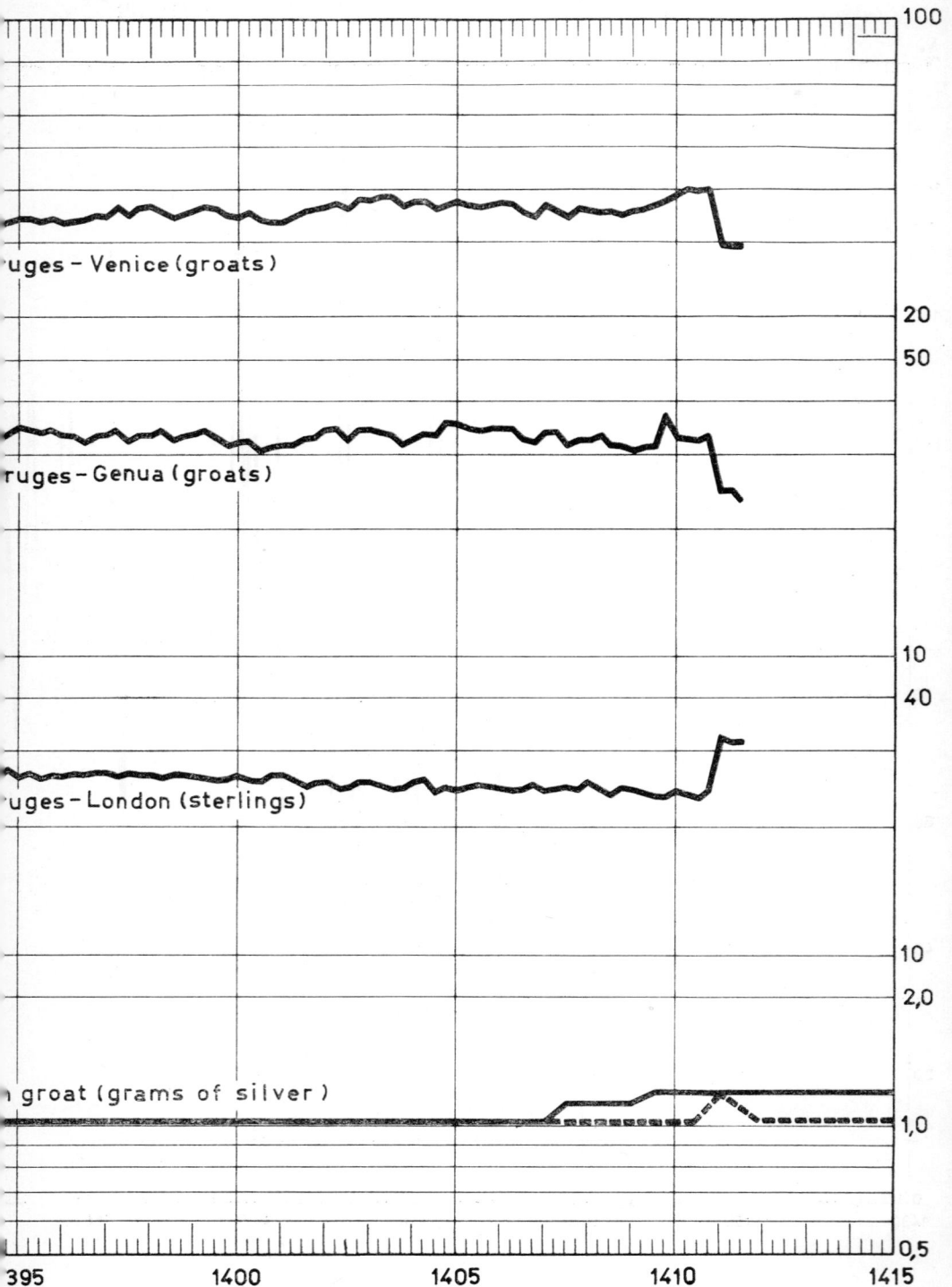

uges – Venice (groats)

ruges – Genua (groats)

uges – London (sterlings)

groat (grams of silver)

395   1400   1405   1410   1415

100
20
50
10
40
10
2,0
1,0
0,5

GRAPH 32

Exchange rates in Bruges: 1384-1412 (ADAT : *correspondence from Bruges*).

Evolution of the official and real weight of fine silver in the Flemish groat : 1380-1415.

GRAPH 33

Exchange rates in Antwerp : 1515-1600.

Evolution of the official weight of fine silver in the Flemish groat : 1515-1600.

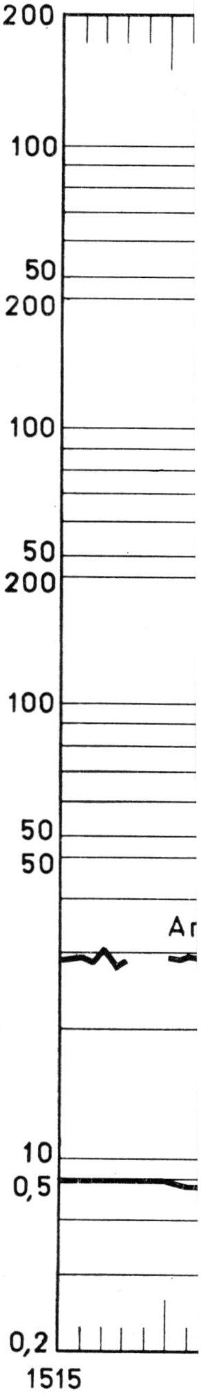

Flandres

Brabant

Ar

200

100

50
200

100

50
200

100

50
50

Ar

10
0,5

0,2

1515

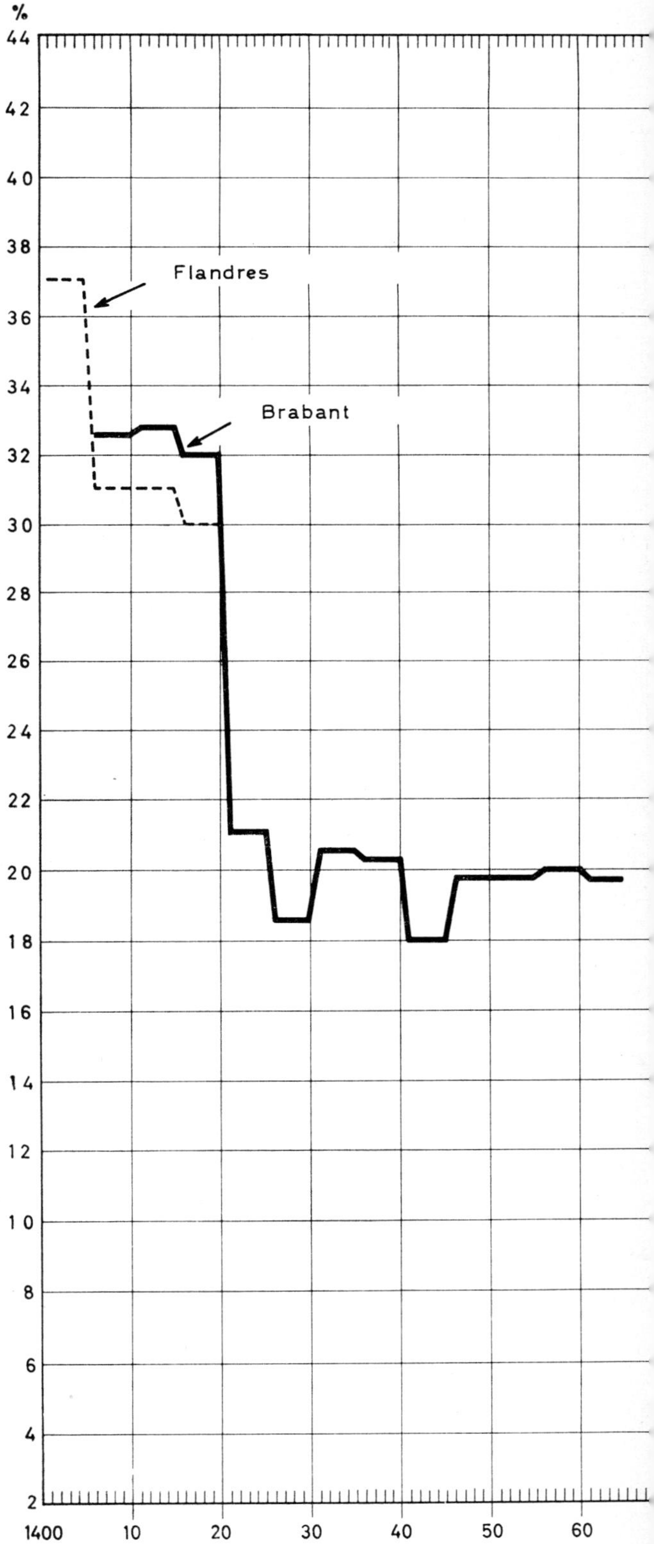

%
44

42

40

38

36

34

32

30

28

26

24

22

20

18

16

14

12

10

8

6

4

2

1400   10   20   30   40   50   60

80

GRAPH 34

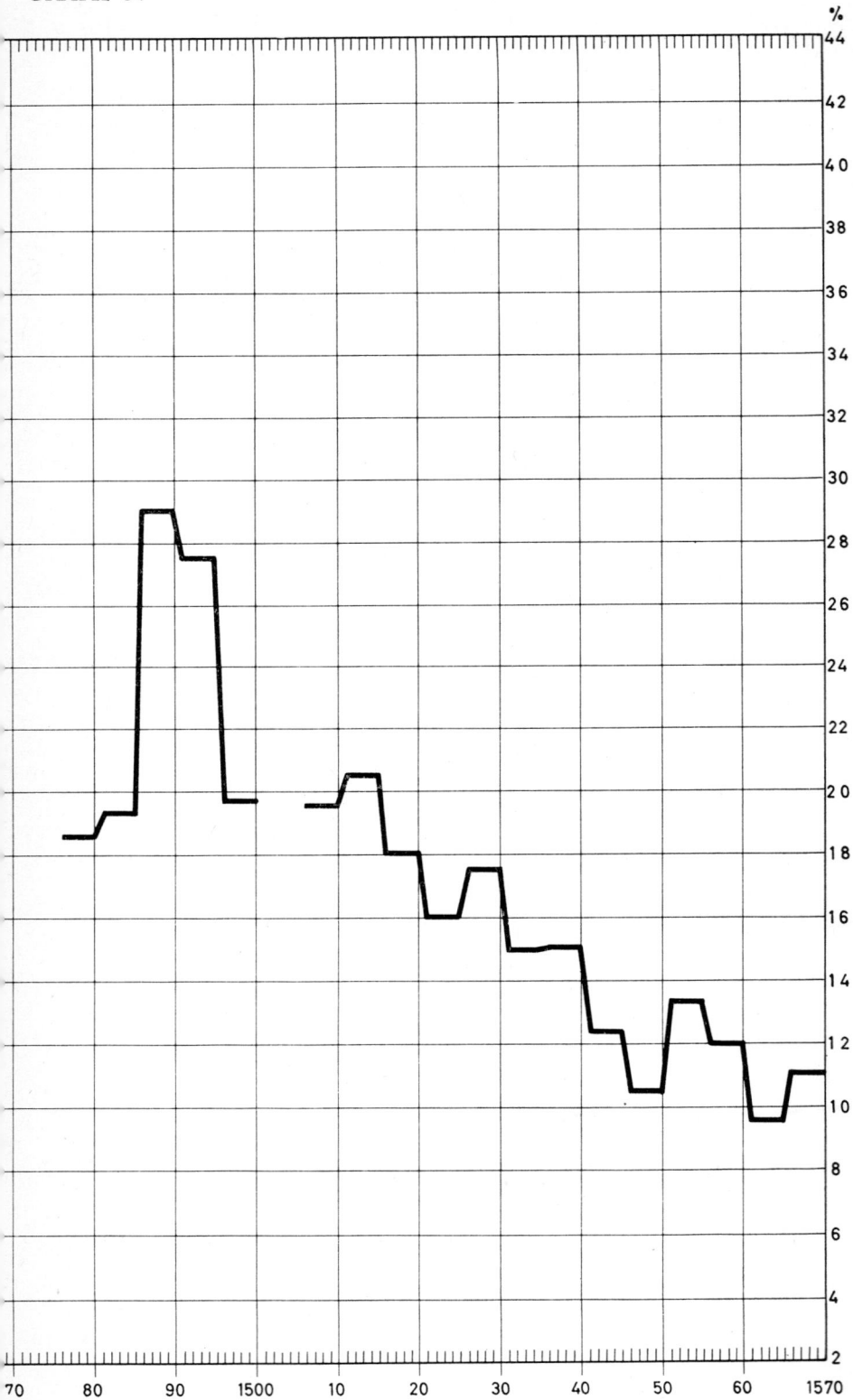

GRAPH 34

Interest rates for short term government loans in Bruges and Antwerp : 1401-1570 (averages per periods of five years).

GRAPH 35

Interest rates for short term government loans on the Antwerp money market 1511-1555 (trimestrial averages).

GRAPH 35

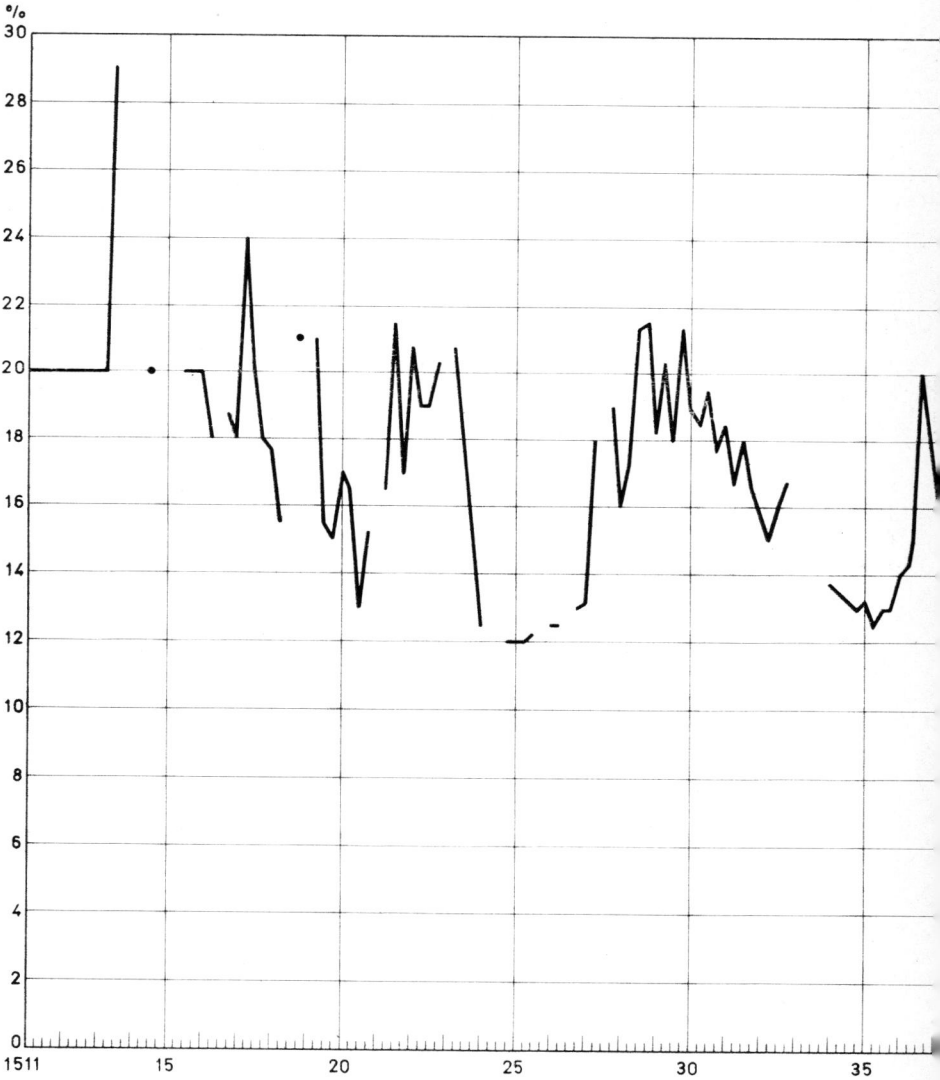

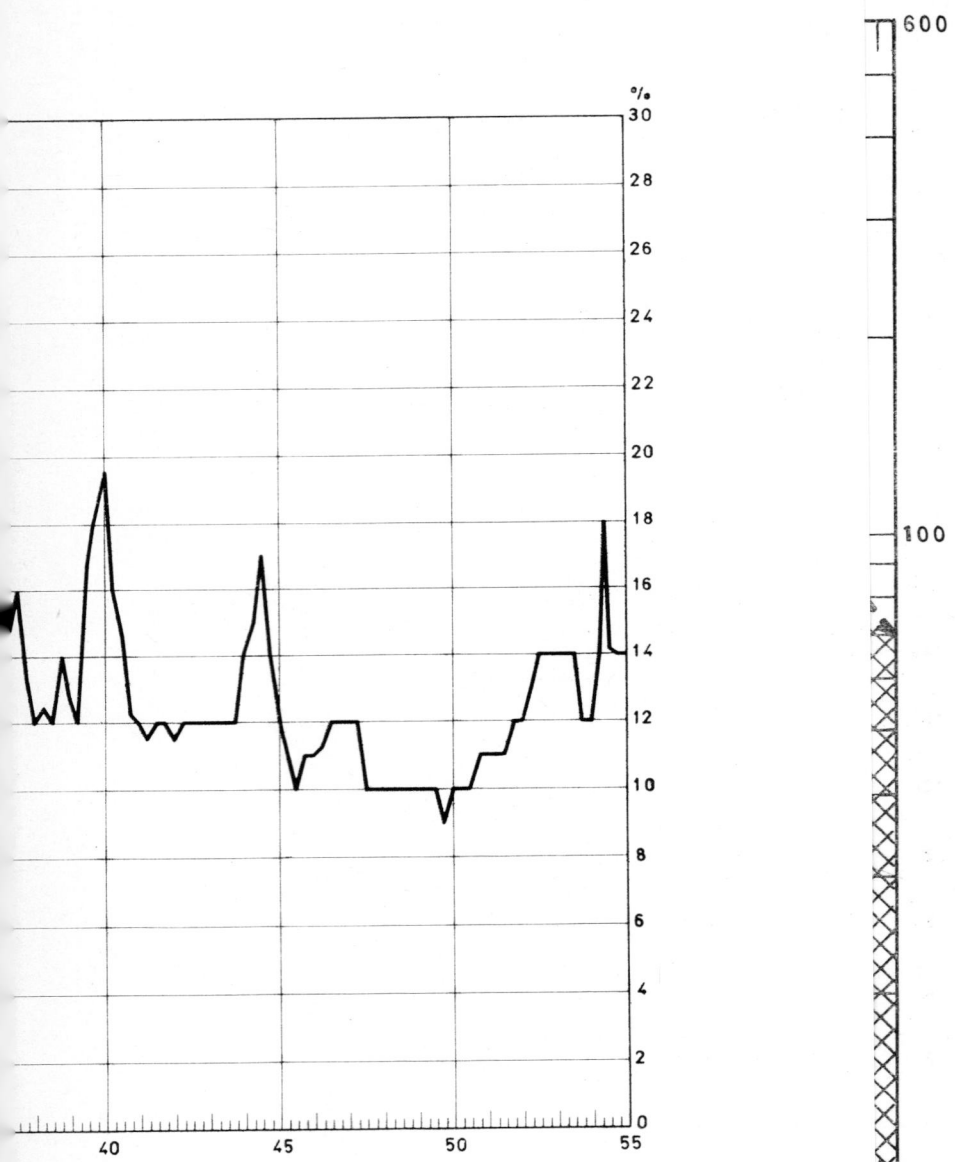

1597

GRAPH 36
Number of poor families supported by the Poor Relief of Lier : 1517-1597.

GRAPH 37

Expenditure, in percentages, by the Infirmary of the Béguinage in Lier on various foodstuffs : 1526-1602.

GRAPH 37

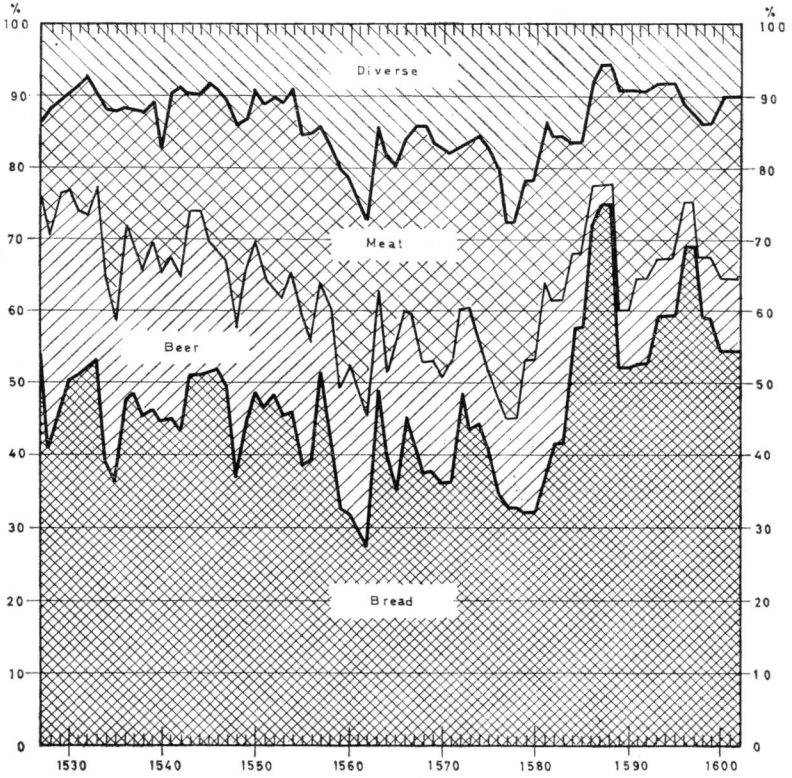

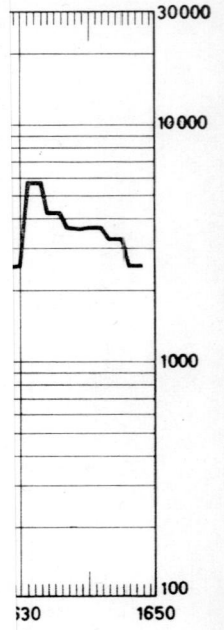

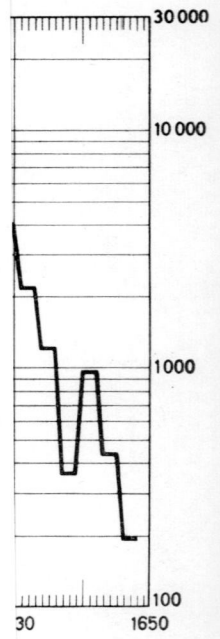

GRAPH 38

Annual ducal income in Brabant money of account from the Cattle toll and Transport toll in Lier : 1403-1648.

GRAPH 39

Comparison of trends of real income of wages earners in Antwerp, Lier and Brussels : 1382-1600 (calculated on logarithmic figures : interquartile moving medians over 13 years with application of the option method).

1 Comparison of purchasing power in litres of rye, of the annual income of masons and mason's labourers in Antwerp and Lier (adjusted by the summer-winter ratio of daily wages and by the employment index of the urban building sector) [a].

2 Comparison of purchasing power in litres of rye, of the income of linen weavers in Brussels and agricultural workers round Lier (adjusted by the employment index of the urban building sector).

3 Comparison of purchasing power of the annual income of an Antwerp mason in litres of rye, in ells of cloth from Weert and in pounds of butter.

[a] For the figures, see vol. I, Part II, appendix 48.

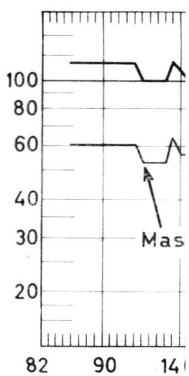

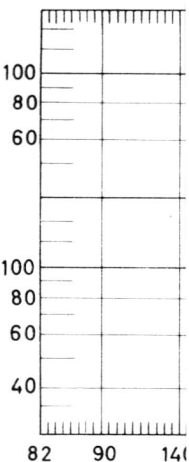

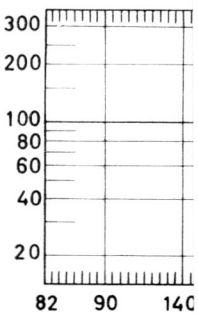

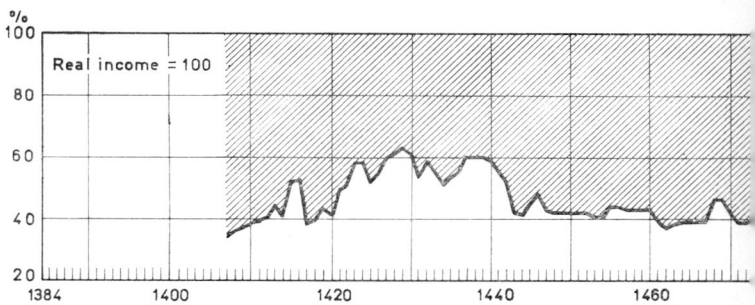

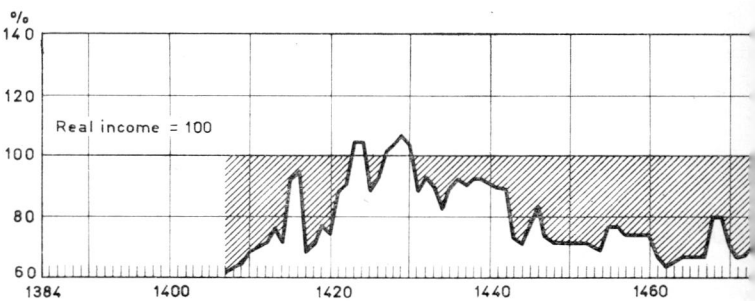

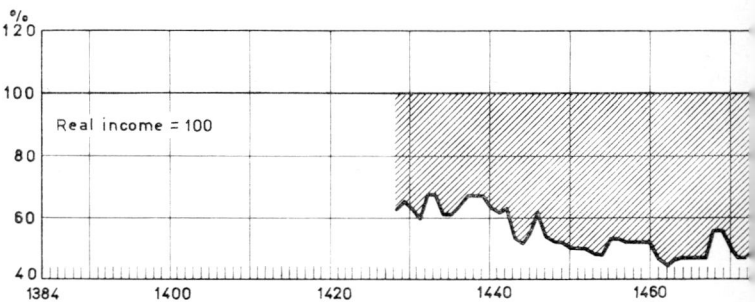

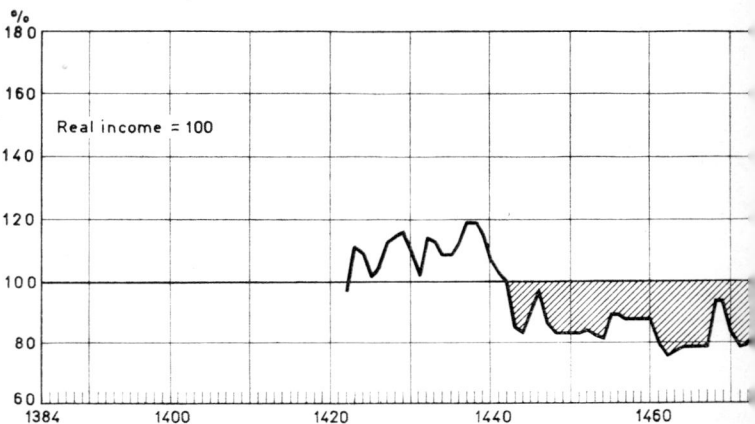

GRAPH 40

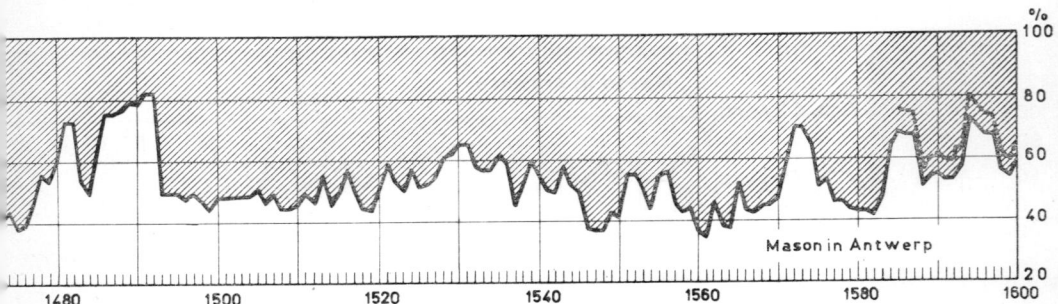

Mason in Antwerp

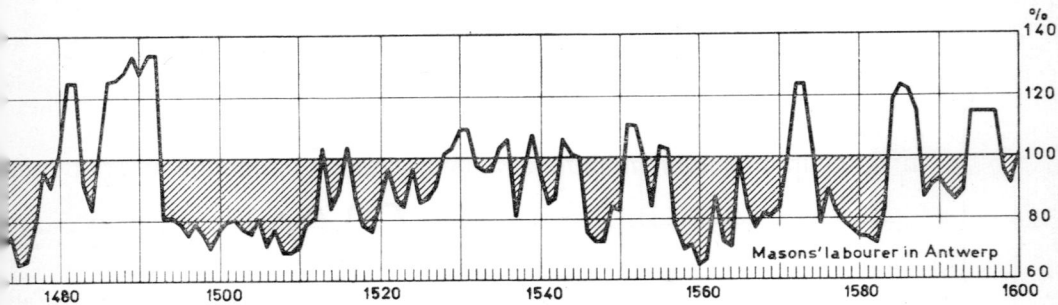

Masons' labourer in Antwerp

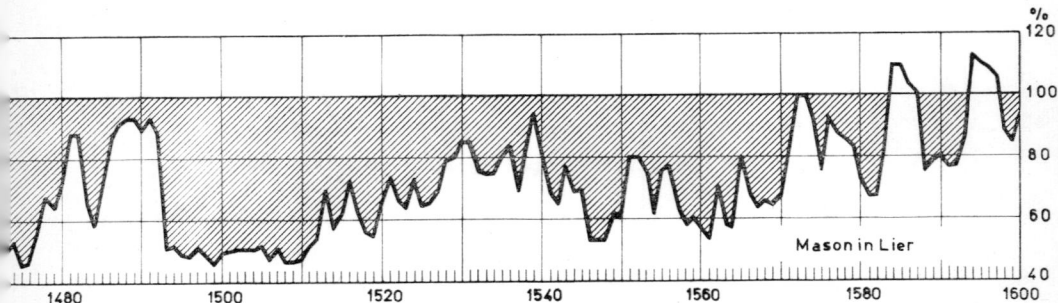

Mason in Lier

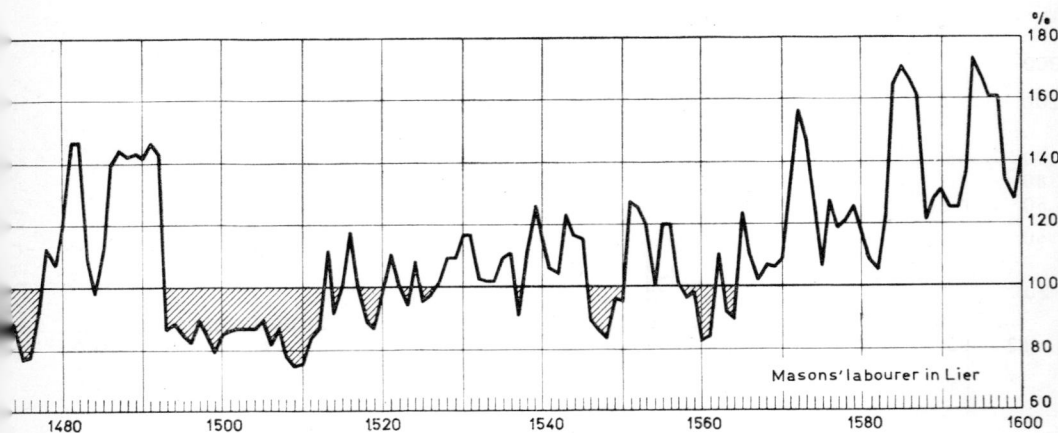

Masons' labourer in Lier

GRAPH 40

Comparison of real income of wage-earners in Antwerp and Lier : 1407-1600.

Margin available for consumption of goods other than essential foodstuffs by a typical family of 5 persons on the basis of real prices and daily wages (with adjustment for employment) [a].

[a] For the figures of the employment index, see vol. I, Part II, appendix 48.

GRAPH 41

1 Yearly ratio between summer daily wages of mason and mason's labourer in Antwerp and Lier : 1399-1600 (the wages of the mason being put at 100).

2 Comparison between the trends of rye prices and mason's daily wages in Antwerp : 1390-1600 (gold equivalents) (moving averages over 13 years of trend figures, the latter being calculated with application of the option method).

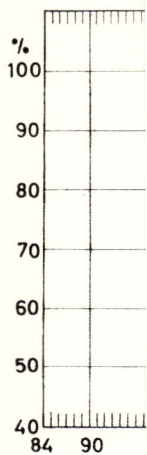

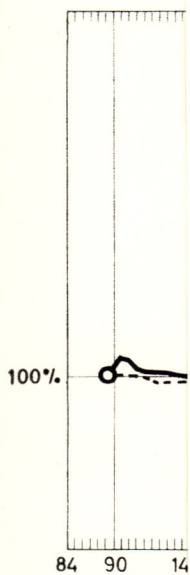

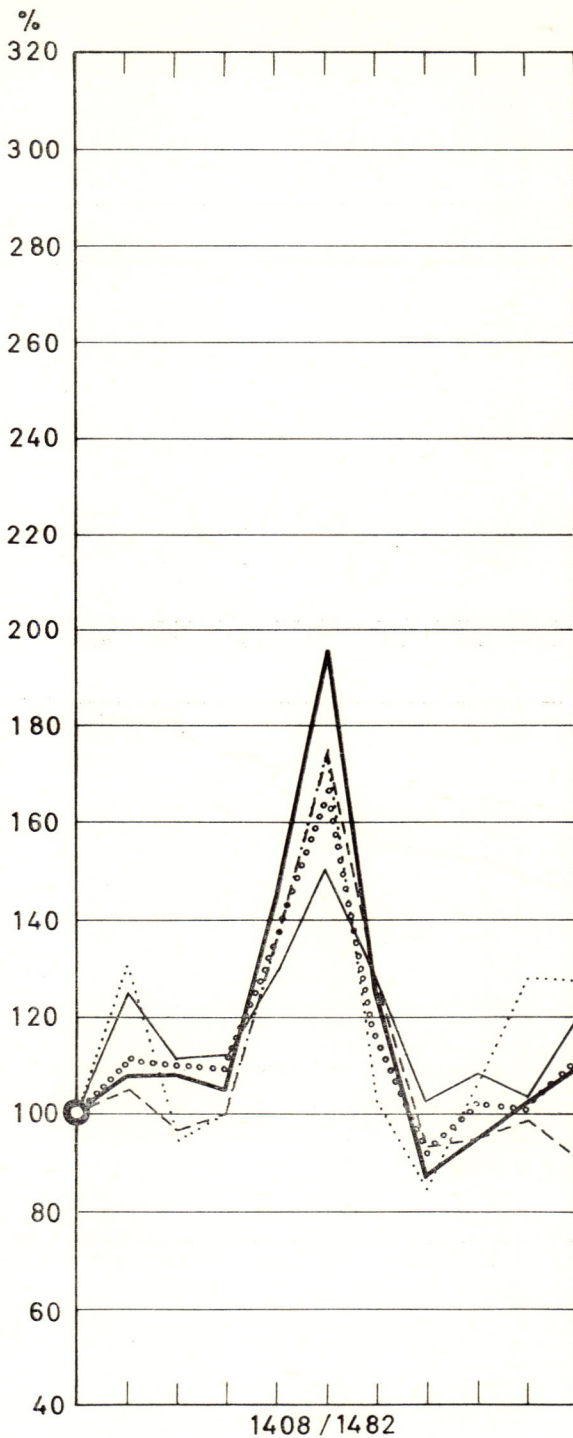

1408 / 1482

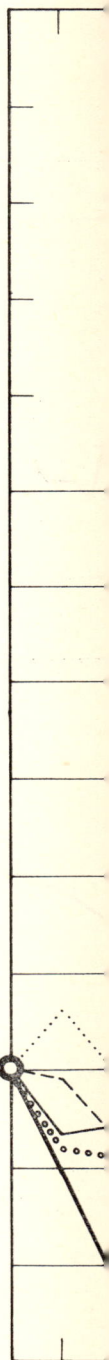

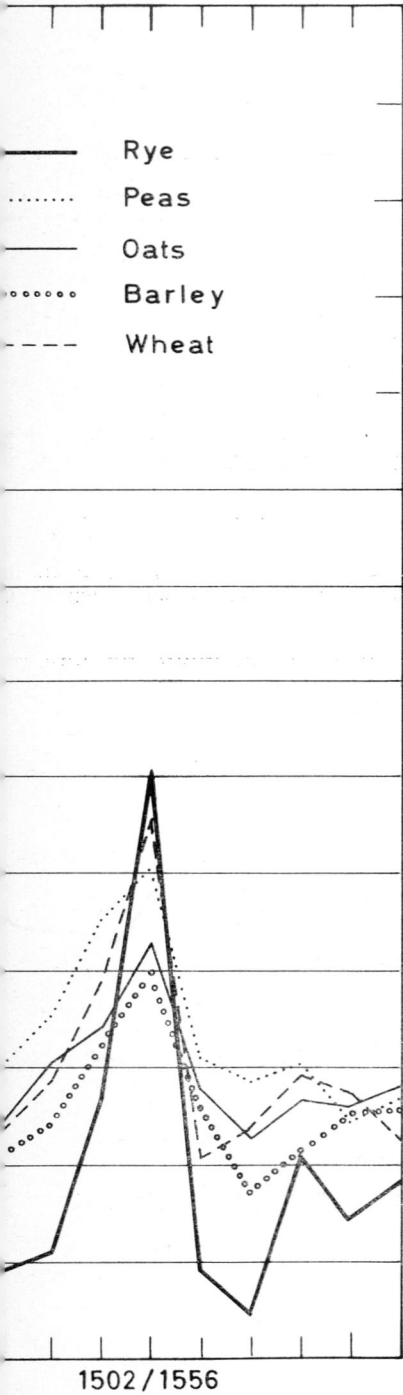

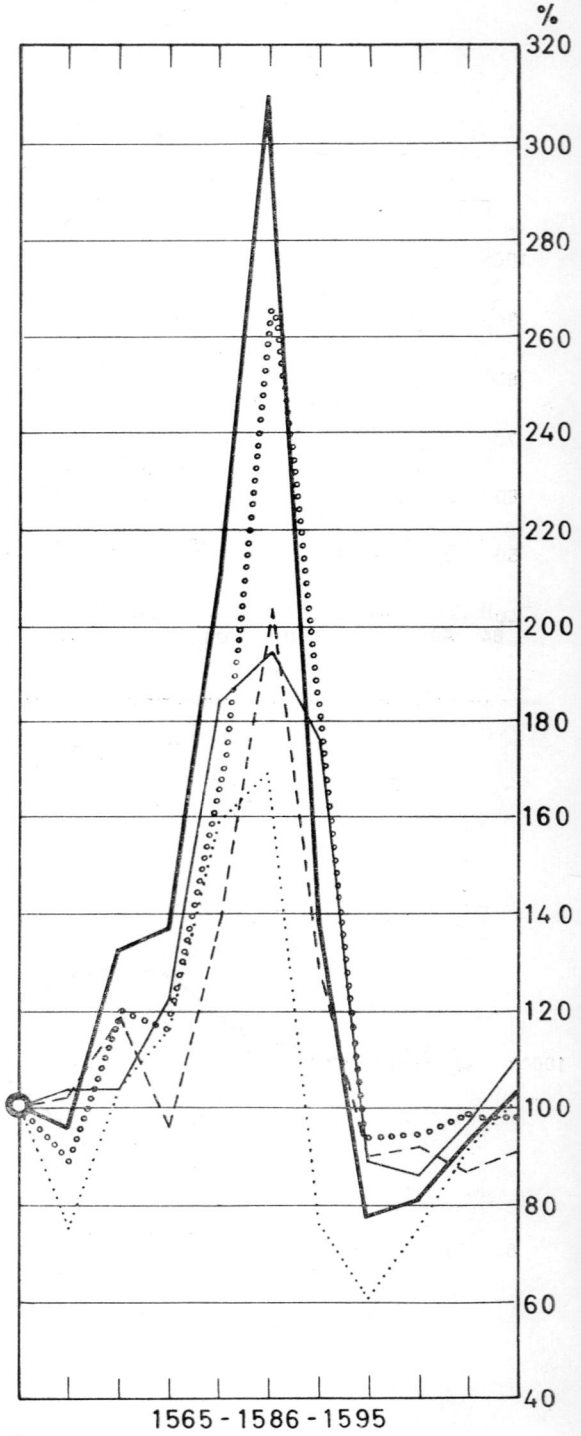

GRAPH 42

Rye
Peas
Oats
Barley
Wheat

1502/1556

1565 - 1586 - 1595

%
320
300
280
260
240
220
200
180
160
140
120
100
80
60
40

GRAPH 42

Crisis behaviour of grain prices in Brabant during three different periods of the fifteenth and sixteenth centuries

(per period: arithmetic means of indices, calculated for each crisis of the period as related to the moving median of the five previous annual data).

GRAPH 43

Crisis behaviour of prices for meat and dairy produce in Brabant during three different periods of the fifteenth and sixteenth centuries (calculation method : see graph 42).

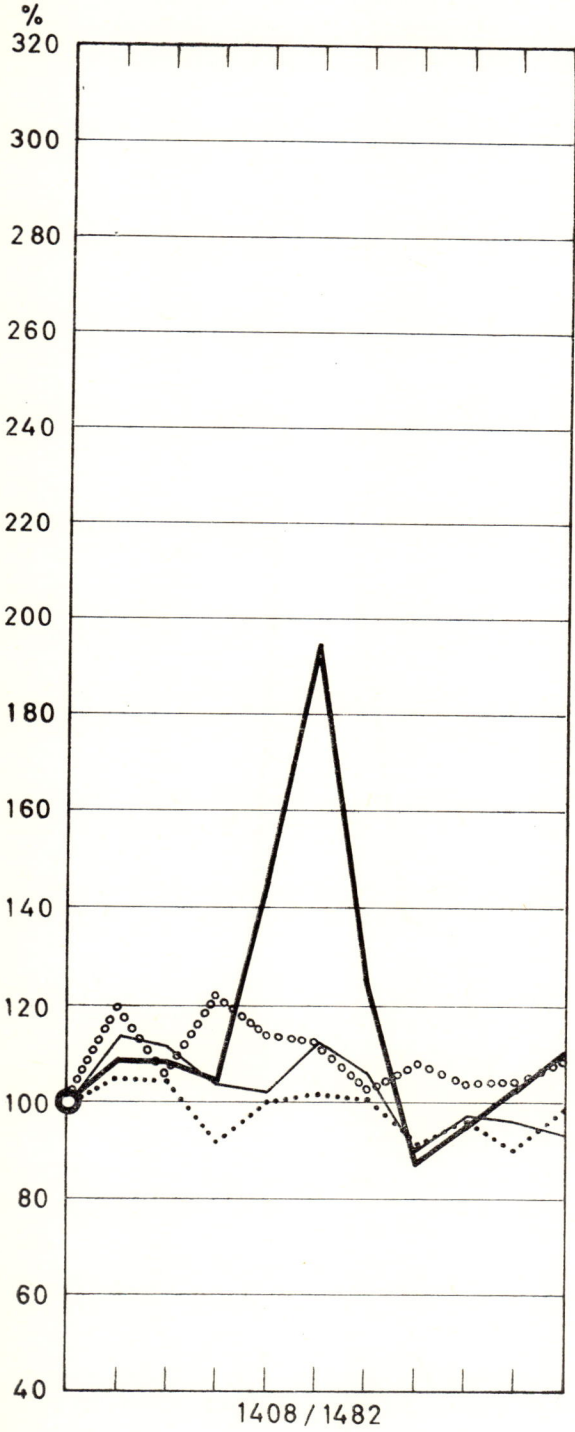

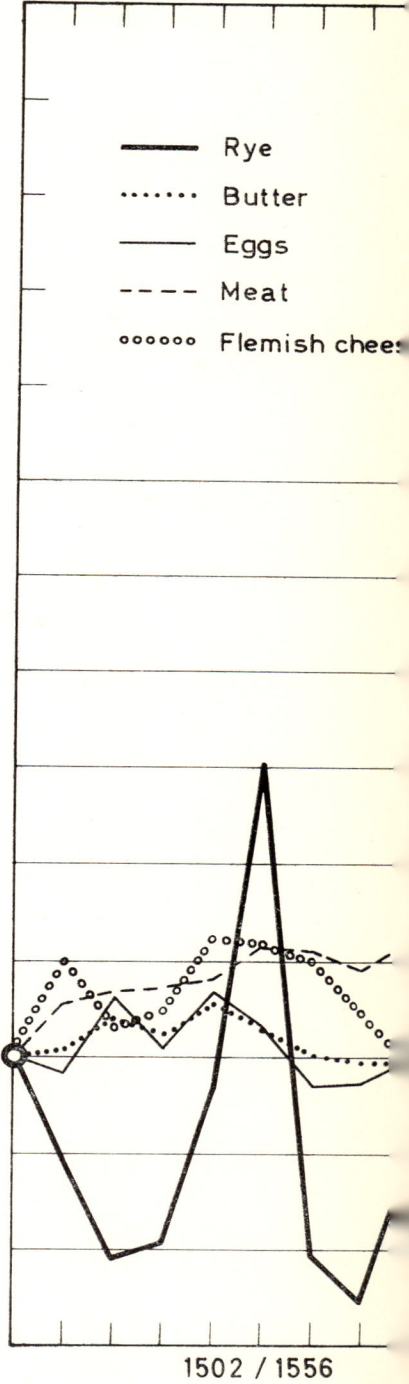

GRAPH 43

Legend:
- ——— Rye
- .... Butter
- ——— Eggs
- – – – Meat
- ∘∘∘∘∘∘ Flemish chee[se]

1408 / 1482

1502 / 1556

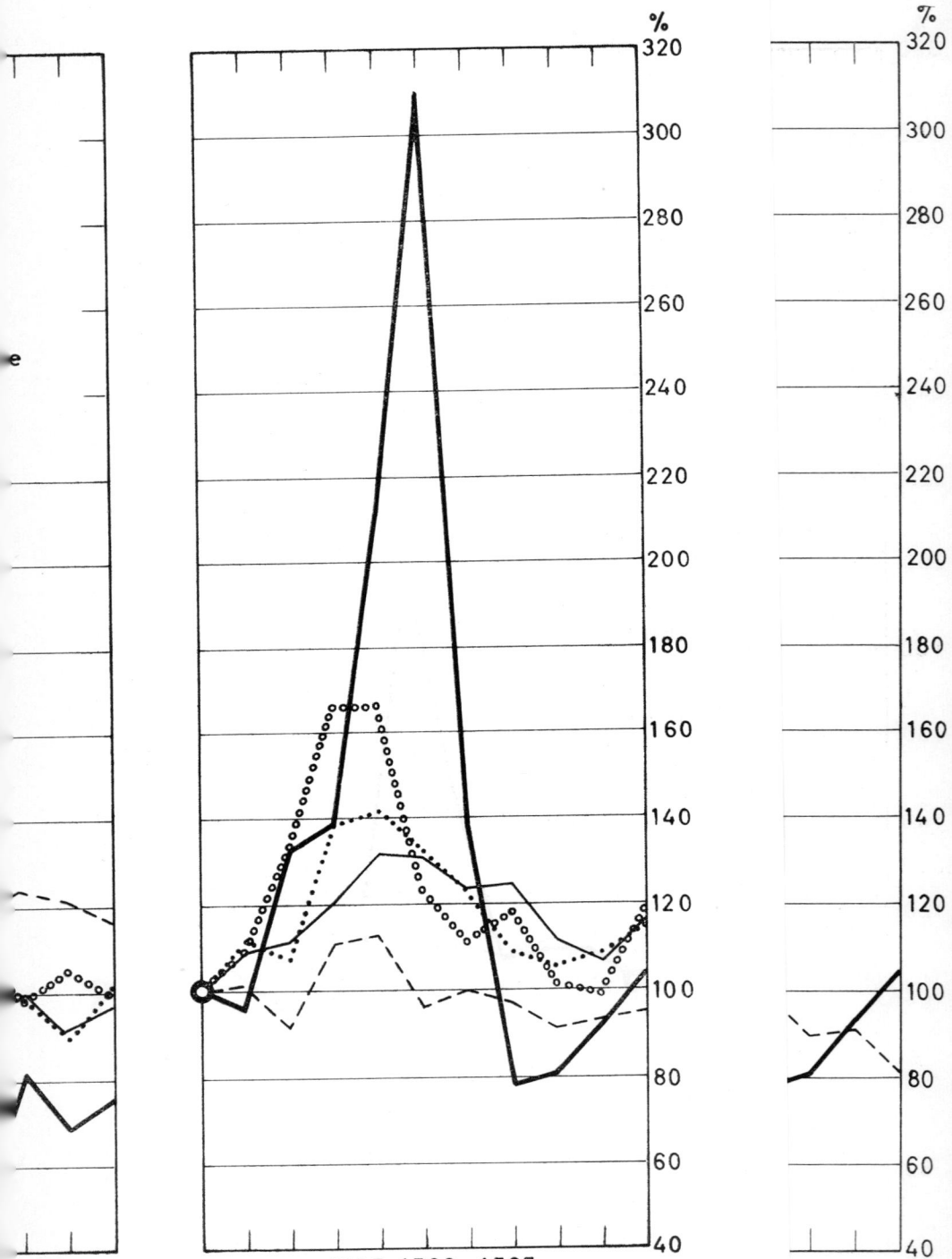

1565 - 1586 - 1595

99

GRAPH 44

Crisis behaviour of prices for industrial crops in Brabant during three different periods of the fifteenth and sixteenth centuries (calculation method : see graph 42).

GRAPH 45

Crisis behaviour of industrial prices in Brabant during three different periods of the fifteenth and sixteenth centuries (calculation method : see graph 42).

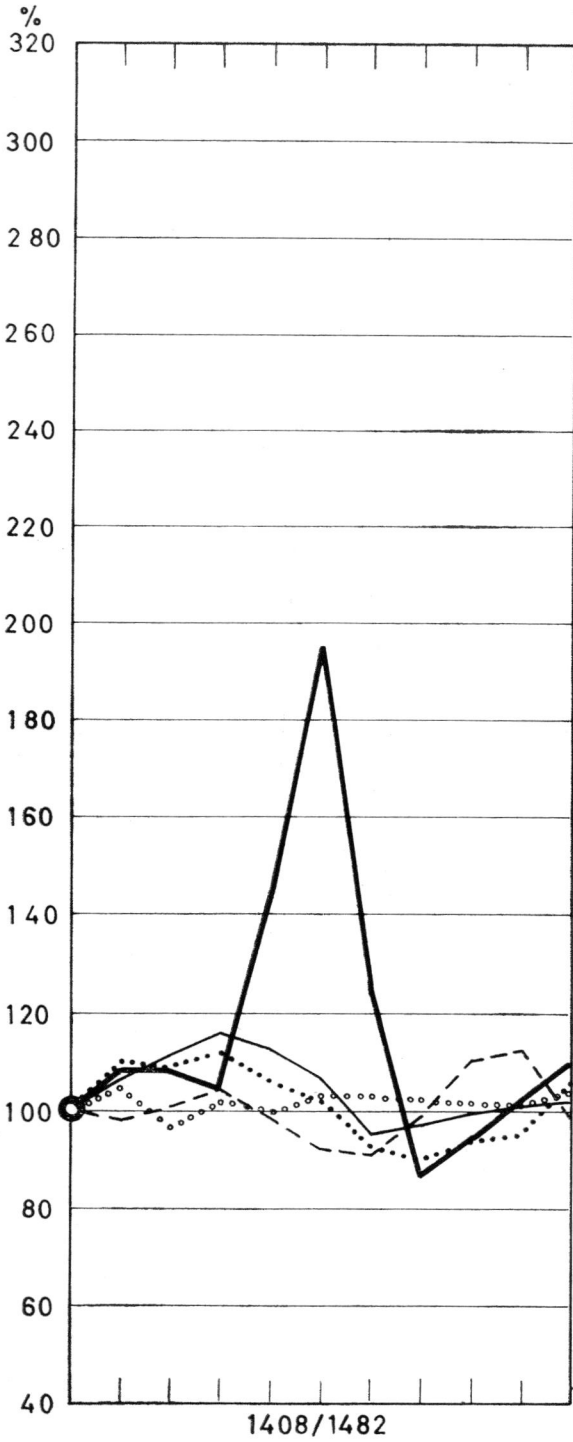

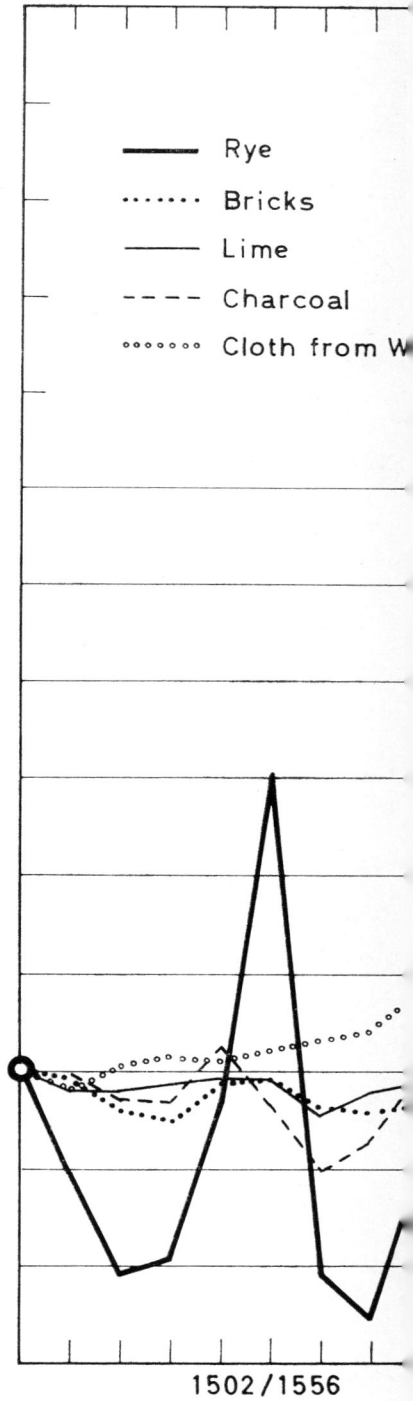

GRAPH 45

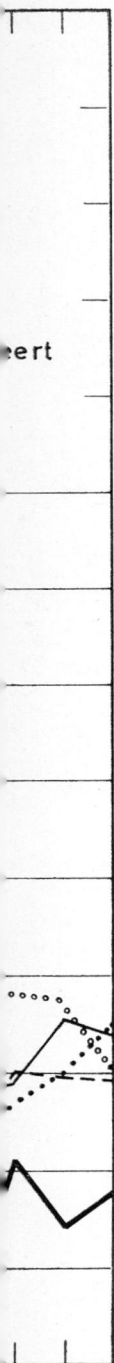

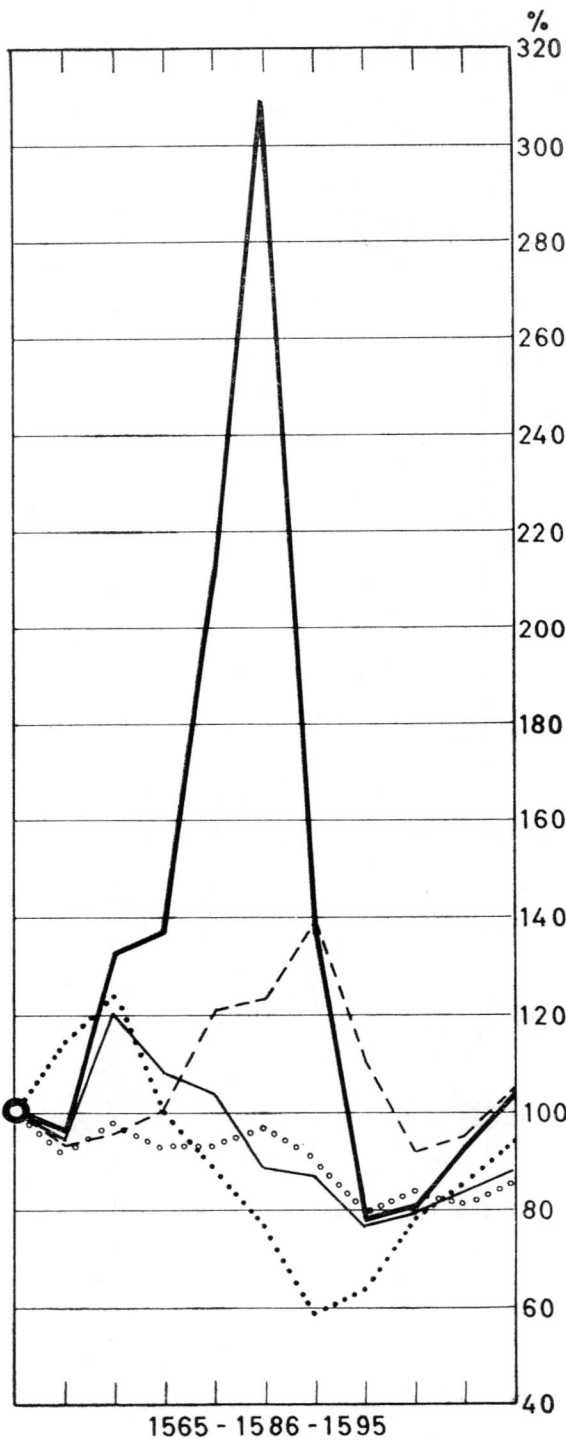

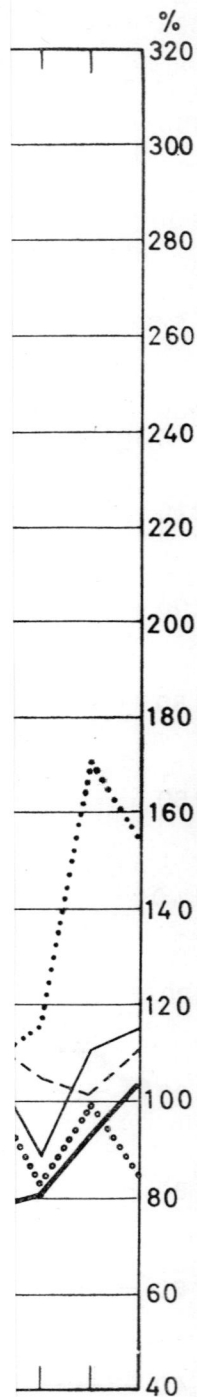

1565 - 1586 -1595

Crisis behaviour of commercial prices in Brabant during three different periods of the fifteenth and sixteenth centuries (calculation method : see graph 42).

GRAPH 47

Crisis behaviour of transit trade, industrial production ([a]) and the money market in Brabant during three different periods of the fifteenth and sixteenth centuries (calculation method : see graph 42).

([a]) Yearly production of Hondschoote says is meant here.

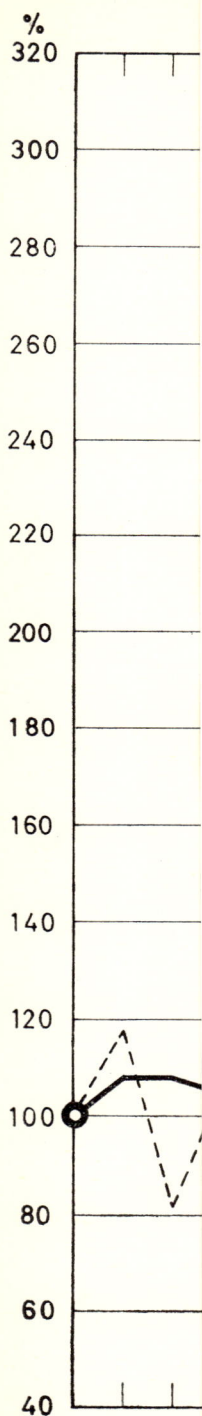

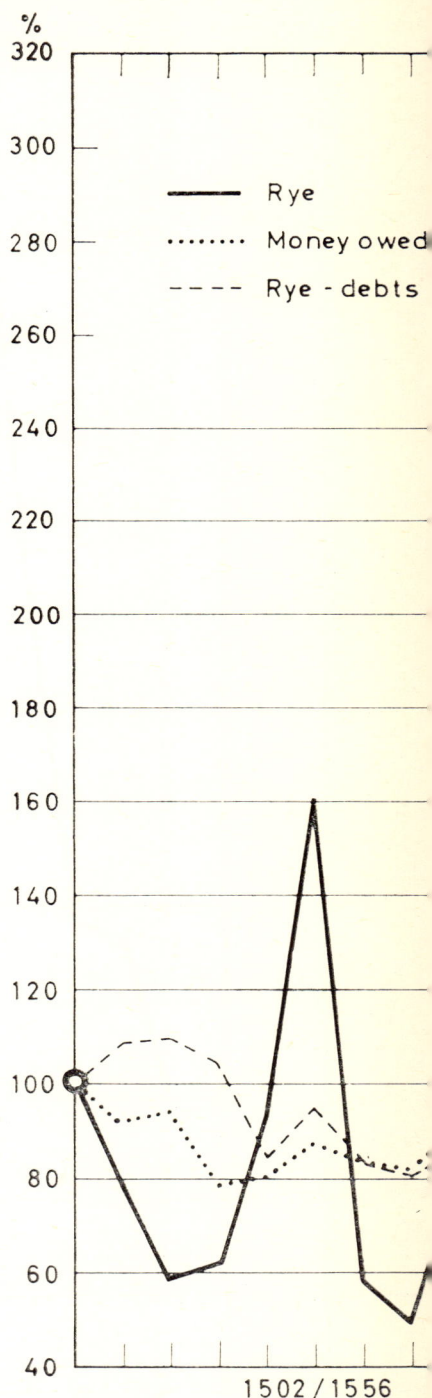

GRAPH 48

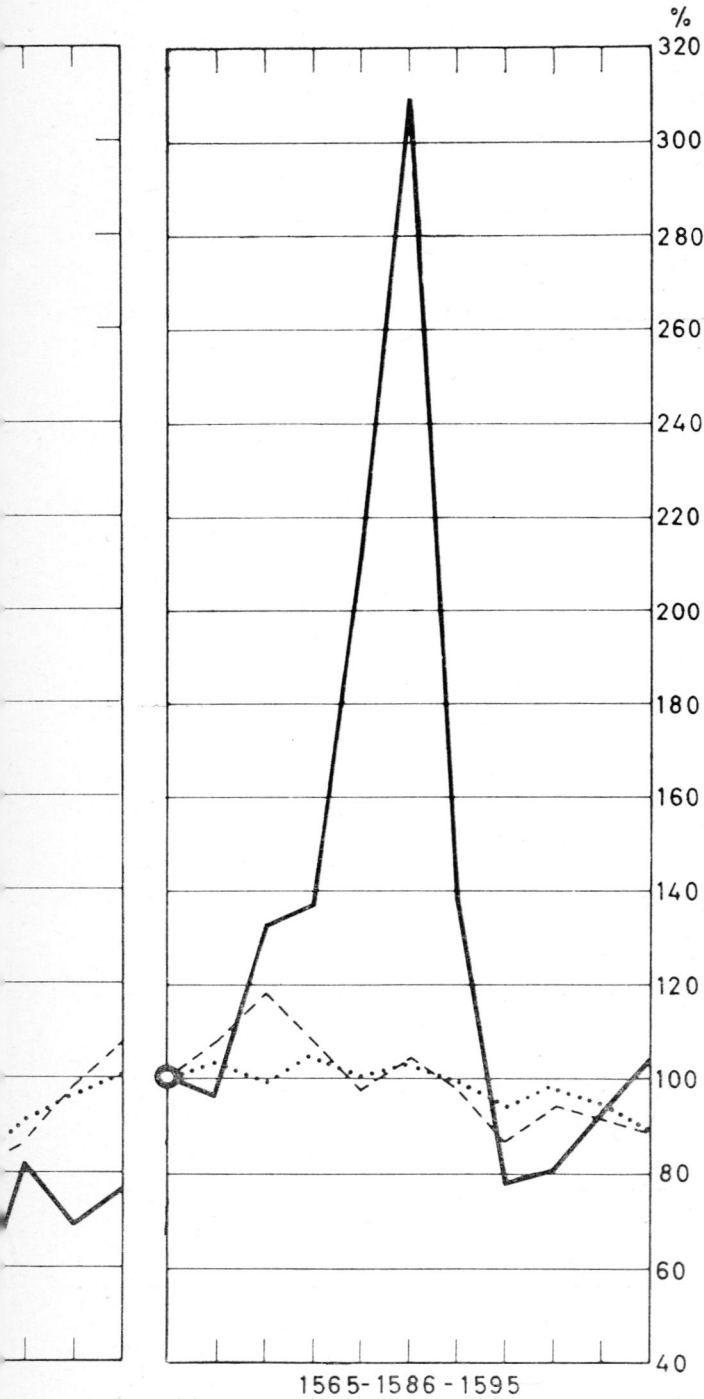

%
320
300
280
260
240
220
200
180
160
140
120
100
80
60
40

1565-1586-1595

Crisis behaviour of debts owed by farmers in Brabant during two different periods of the fifteenth and sixteenth centuries (calculation method : see graph 42).

GRAPH 49

Crisis behaviour of daily and piece wages of skilled (ᵃ) wage-earners in Brabant during three different periods of the fifteenth and sixteenth centuries (calculation method : see graph 42).

(ᵃ) For Antwerp the wages of master-masons were used from 1586 onwards.

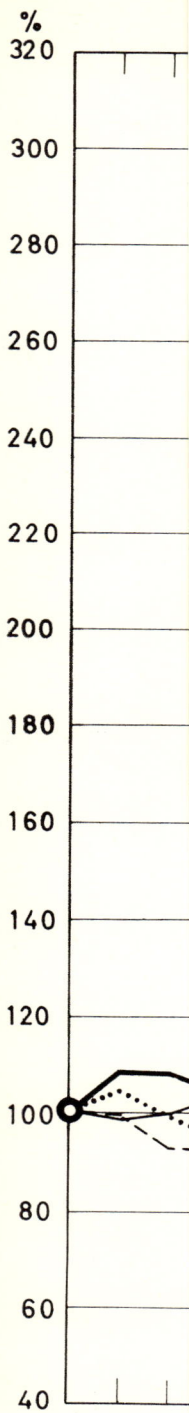

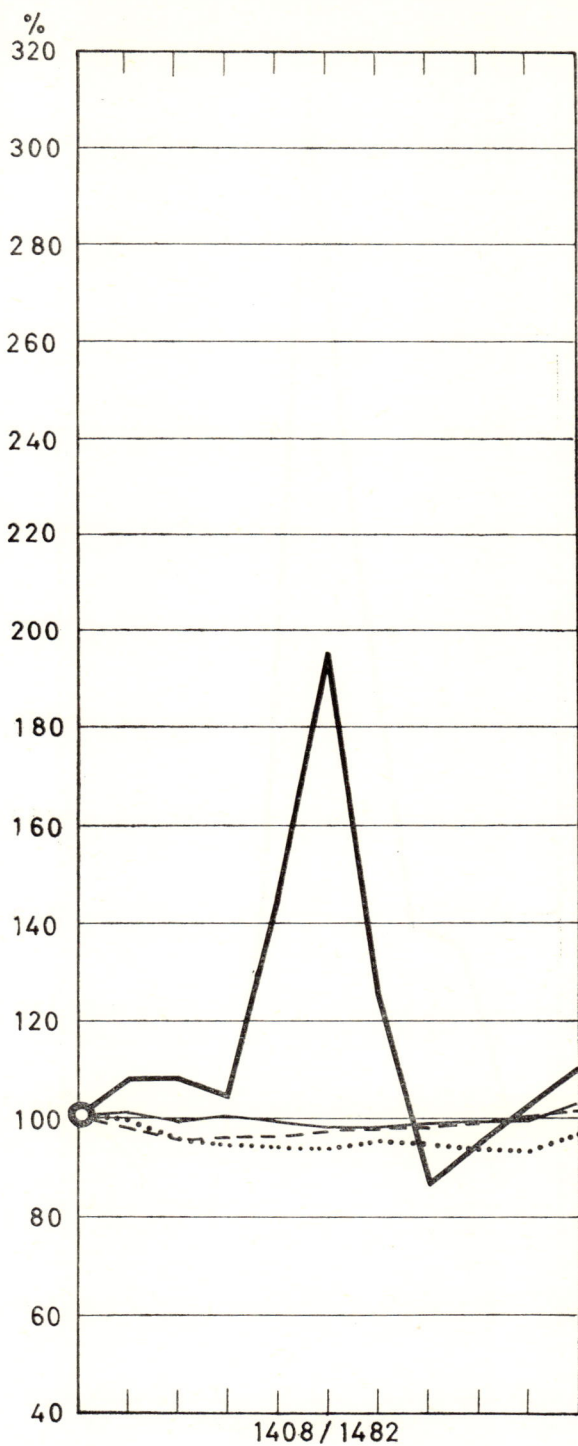

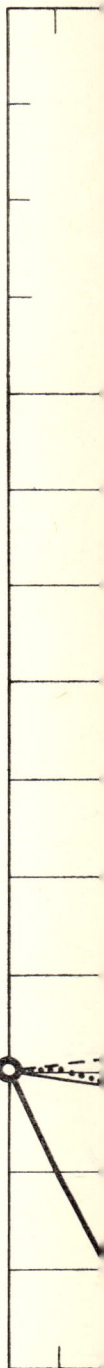

320 %

1408 / 1482

112

GRAPH 50

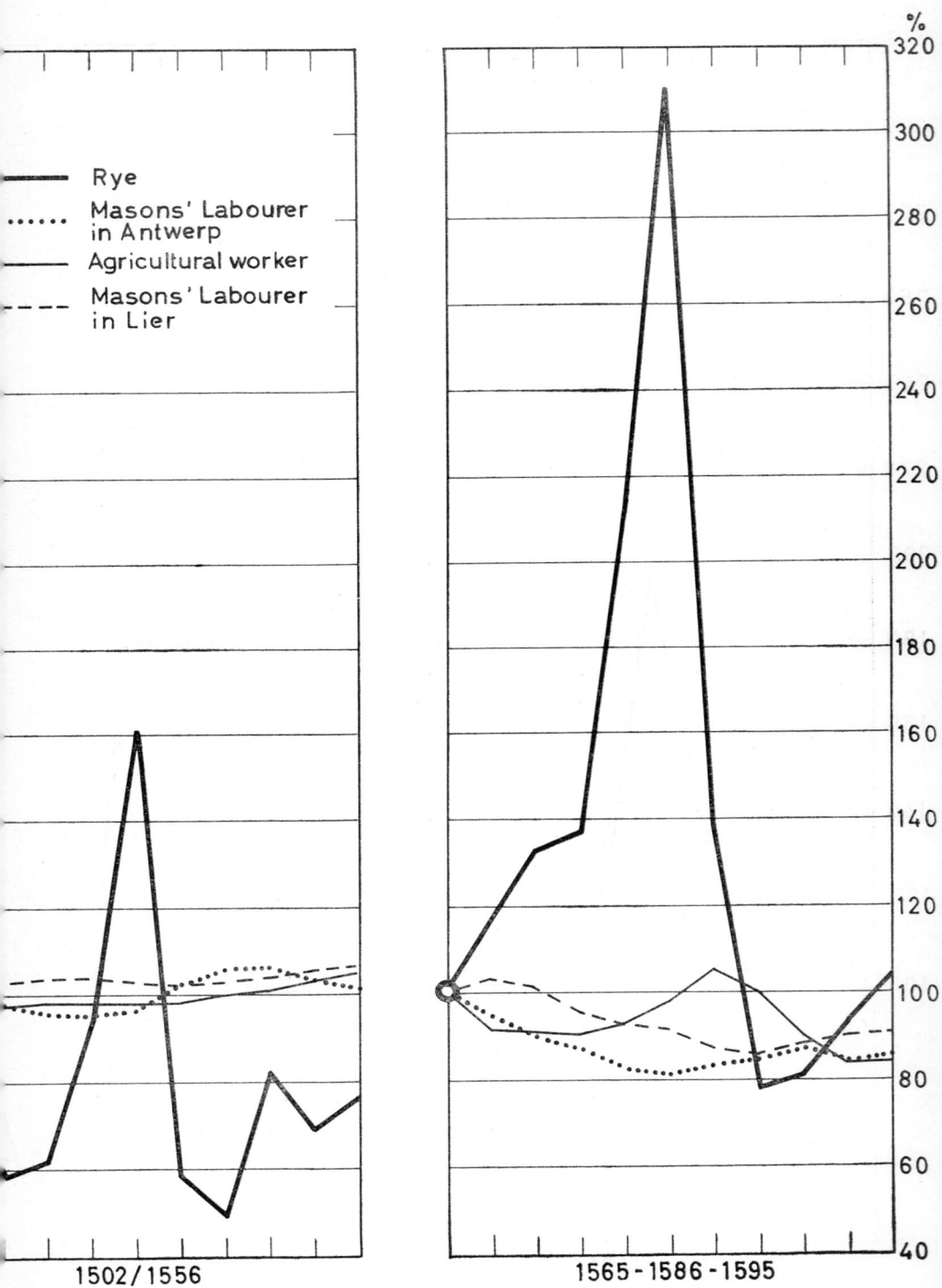

%
320

300

280

260

240

220

200

180

160

140

120

100

80

60

40

Rye

Masons' Labourer
in Antwerp

Agricultural worker

Masons' Labourer
in Lier

1502 / 1556

1565 - 1586 - 1595

GRAPH 50

Crisis behaviour of daily and piece wages ([a]) of unskilled wage-earners in Brabant during three periods of the fifteenth and sixteenth centuries (calculation method : see graph 42).

([a]) The agricultural workers were in the rural area eastward of Lier.

GRAPH 51

Trimestrial evolution of wheat prices, marriages and conceptions in Lier : 1582-1600 (moving averages over three terms).

GRAPH 51

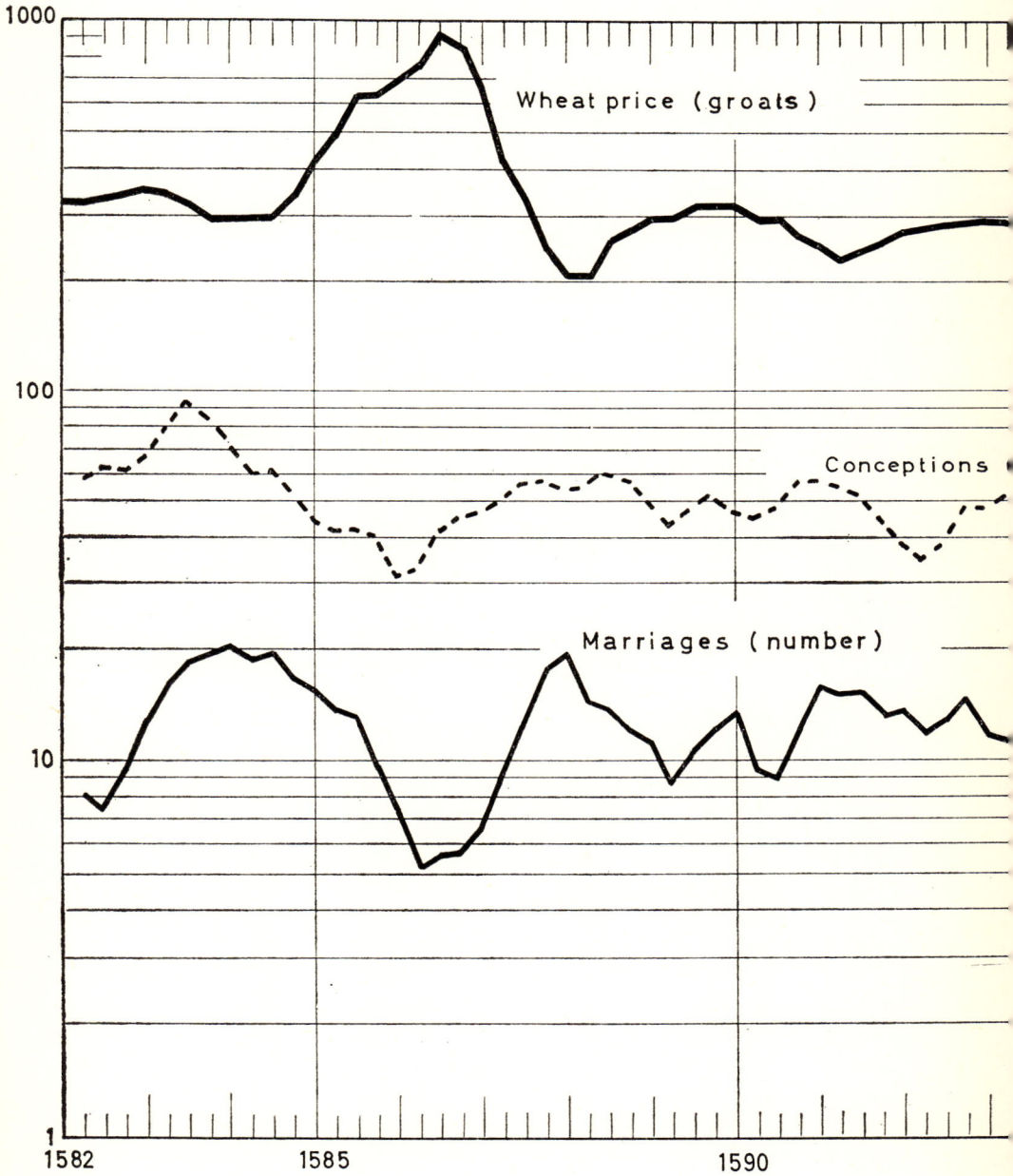

Wheat price (groats)

Conceptions

Marriages (number)

1000

100

10

1

1582   1585   1590

GRAPH 52

Comparison of price trends in Brabant : 1391-1600 (calculation on logarithmic figures : interquartile moving medians over 13 years with application of the option method).

— comparison between nominal prices (Brabant money of account) and its silver and gold equivalents.

— comparison of different prices as related to rye prices, the year 1450 being equalized for all series (silver equivalents).

PART II

INDICES OF VOLUMES I AND II

INDEX OF PERSONS [1] AND PLACES

A

Aachen, **II**, 126, 373.

Aarschot, **I**, 295, 547; **II**, 10, 64, 69, 99.

Abbéville, **I**, 24 (n. 61).

Adriatic coast, **II**, 182.

Affaitadi (*merchant family*), **II**, 129, 131, 323, 325, 343 (n. 60).

Africa, **II**, 105, 224, 257, 412, 423.

Alexandria, **II**, 127, 153, 154.

Alfen, **I**, 517 (n. 1); **III**, 36.

Alost, **I**, 228, 229, 233; **II**, 32 (n. 7), 116, 138, 170, 188, 189, 254, 298 (n. 45), 301.

Alps, **II**, 82, 154, 155.

Alsace, **II**, 63, 76.

Alva (*Fernando Alvarez de Toledo, duke of*), **II**, 236-239, 241, 253, 366.

Ambrosi (*Deo*), **II**, 22.

America, **I**, 56; **II**, 124, 125, 129, 146, 159, 177, 178, 190, 201, 202, 204-206, 213, 223, 265, 273 (n. 21), 281, 317, 318, 363, 377, 407, 418.

Amsterdam, **I**, 74, 76, 85, 86, 88, 89, 91-93, 104 (n. 152), 109 (n. 8), 119, 121, 155, 522; **II**, 120-122, 157, 158, 171, 179 (n. 195), 213, 217-219, 222, 225, 229, 231 (n. 139), 232, 235, 251, 257, 262, 263, 273, 319 (n. 54), 322, 330, 359 (n. 136),

366, 367, 392 (n. 9), 402 (n. 36).

Ancona, **II**, 156, 180.

Andalusia, **I**, 288; **II**, 179.

Anjou (*duke of*), **II**, 258.

Anthony of Burgundy (*duke of Brabant and Limburg*), **I**, 111 (n. 16); **II**, 33, 39, 57, 87.

Antwerp, passim.

Arendonk, **II**, 63 (n. 10), 69 (n. 46), 99, 103 (n. 87).

Arlon, **II**, 265 (n. 160).

Armentières, **II**, 132 (n. 109), 137, 175, 185, 187, 323, 329, 338, 359.

Arnemuiden, **I**, 96, 102; **II**, 38, 79.

Arnolfini (*merchant family*) **II**, 84, 296 (n. 34).

Arras, **II**, 101, 186.

Artois, **I**, 108 (n. 4); **II**, 28 (n. 146), 101, 120, 122 (n. 51), 217 (n. 51), 231 (n. 139), 301.

Asinari (*Lombard family*), **II**, 58, 86.

Asse, **I**, 228, 517 (n. 1).

Assenede, **II**, 175 (n. 175), 307.

Ath, **II**, 69 (n. 46).

Atlantic, **II**, 127, 130, 136, 179 (n. 198), 223, 317, 318, 423.

Atlantic islands, **I**, 306; **II**, 77, 105, 130, 318.

Audenaarde, **I**, 55, 233; **II**, 15, 38, 118, 138, 175, 188, 190, 215, 229,

---

[1] The names of persons are printed in italics.

247, 256, 258, 259, 276 (n. 39), 303,
306, 323 (n. 79), 329, 380.
Augsburg, **I**, 68 (n. 24); **II**, 54
(n. 153), 149, 159, 205 (n. 361),
247 (n. 9), 266, 321 (n. 60).
Aunis, **I**, 287, 288.
Austruweel, **I**, 557.

Aveiro, **I**, 288.
Averbode (Abbey of), **I**, 52; **II**, 296
(n. 34), 361 (n. 140).
Avignon, **II**, 314.
Axel, **I**, 96, 288; **II**, 138.
Azores, **I**, 306; **II**, 130, 179, 423.

B

Bacheliers (*merchant*), **II**, 226.
Bailleul, **II**, 175, 258.
Balbani (*merchant family*), **II**, 111.
Baldini (*merchant family*), **II**, 110.
Baltic, **I**, 24 (n. 61), 56; **II**, 12, 24
(n. 116), 26 (n. 135), 40, 45, 68, 80,
102, 120, 121, 146, 150, 156, 157,
158, 160 (n. 111), 164, 165, 171,
172, 184, 185, 192, 209, 211, 217-
219, 224, 225, 229, 239, 246, 250,
251, 257, 278, 282, 302, 312, 313,
314, 318, 327, 377, 392 (n. 10),
399 (n. 28), 402, 417, 431, 434.
Barbary, **II**, 322.
Barcelona, **II**, 241.
Bäsweiler, **II**, 9.
Beauce, **II**, 101, 120.
Beers, **III**, 36.
Bel (*Jan*), **II**, 350 (n. 88).
Bellarminus (*Robertus*), **II**, 353.
Berchem (near Antwerp), **II**, 249.
Berg (*lord of*), **II**, 39.
Bergeik, **III**, 36.
Bergen-op-Zoom, **I**, 61, 510, 514
(n. 8), 517 (n. 1), 519, 520, 547; **II**,
22, 23, 25, 26 (n. 130), 27, 28
(n. 144), 29, 33, 37, 46, 49, 52, 55
(n. 158), 59, 63 (n. 10), 71, 72
(n. 67), 76 (n. 89), 79, 80, 99 (n. 62),
100, 103 (n. 87), 104, 106, 107,
108, 110, 119 (n. 29), 136, 137,

165, 184, 323, 328, 329, 356, 357,
358; **III**, 65.
Bergues-Saint-Winnoc, **II**, 66 (n. 27),
187.
Berkel, **II**, 298 (n. 43).
Berlaar, **III**, 35.
Berlicum, **II**, 229.
Bernardi (*merchant family*), **II**, 110.
Bertout (*Jean*) (*merchant*), **II**, 342
(n. 54).
Besançon, **II**, 180, 182, 202, 205, 221,
360; **III**, 79.
Betekom, **I**, 517 (n. 1).
Beukels (*Willem*), **I**, 277, 278.
Beveland, **II**, 167.
Biervliet, **I**, 277, 288; **II**, 274.
Biscay, **II**, 217 (n. 51).
Bodin (*Jean*), **I**, 116, 121, 122.
Boechout, **I**, 477.
Boelman (*merchant*), **II**, 349 (n. 78).
Bonvisi (*merchant family*), **II**, 266
(n. 171).
Boom, **I**, 99, 257, 262; **II**, 138.
Bordeaux, **II**, 322.
Borgerhout, **II**, 249.
Borsbeek, **II**, 248 (n. 21); **III**, 35.
Boshoven (near Alfen), 517 (n. 1).
Bosnia, **II**, 311.
Boulogne, **I**, 24 (n. 61).
Bourgneuf, **I**, 287, 288.
Bouvignes, **II**, 119 (n. 29).

Bouwel, **II**, 245 (n. 2).
Braakman, **II**, 167.
Brabant, passim.
Brabants (*Gielis*), **I**, 40 (n. 107).
Brecht, **III**, 36.
Breda, **I**, 288, 547; **II**, 69, 100, 337.
Bremen, **I**, 228 (n. 4); **II**, 74, 216, 217, 262.
Brenner Pass, **II**, 124.
Bresser (*Catrina*), **II**, 348 (n. 78).
Brest, **II**, 78 (n. 101).
Breughel (*Pieter, the elder*), **II**, 176, 305.
Brill, **II**, 240, 241, 245, 250, 263, 417, 424, 430.
Brittany, **I**, 287, 295; **II**, 50, 78, 115 (n. 12), 183, 224, 318.
Broechem, **I**, 238 (n. 1); **III**, 36.
Brouage, **I**, 287, 288.
Bruges, **I**, 8, 58, 73-75, 85, 104, 150 294, 306, 525, 526, 553; **II**, 11, 12, 14, 15, 18-30, 38, 46, 49-58, 66 (n. 27), 73-78, 79 (n. 111), 84, 87, 96-98, 101, 103-107, 109-111, 119, 120, 131, 133, 136, 140, 157, 158 (n. 96), 164, 179, 184, 187, 188, 190, 192, 219, 223, 230, 254, 258, 296 (n. 34), 309 (n. 4), 311 (n. 14), 312 (n. 17), 313-315, 323, 327, 328, 330, 341 (n. 49), 343, 355, 361, 369, 378, 429; **III**, 76, 77, 81.
Brussels, passim.
Buggenhout, **II**, 319 (n. 54).
Burgos, **II**, 221 (n. 74), 237 (n. 176), 239, 281.
Burgundy, **I**, 8 (n. 20), 34, 61, 68, 103, 108, 109, 110 (n. 11), 229; **II**, 57, 62, 67, 70, 94, 314, 358 (n. 130), 361.
Buvrinnes, **I**, 229.

C

Cadiz, **I**, 288.
Caen, **II**, 83.
Calais, **II**, 11, 37, 40 (n. 56), 46, 56, 101 (n. 73), 252, 262, 338, 342 (n. 54).
Calcutta, **I**, 306; **II**, 125, 154.
Cambi (*merchant family*), **II**, 110.
Cambrai, **II**, 186, 188.
Campi (*merchant family*), **II**, 84.
Canaries, **I**, 306; **II**, 130, 179, 192, 224, 322, 423.
Cantelo, **II**, 342 (n. 54).
Castile, **I**, 61; **II**, 179, 180, 201, 206, 221-223, 237, 366; **III**, 30, 31, 79.
Castillo, **II**, 212.
Cavalli (*Marino*), **II**, 415 (n. 13).
Chaam, **III**, 36.
Chalon-sur-Saône, **II**, 51, 59, 77, 124, 314, 361, 430.
Champagne, **I**, 73; **II**, 12, 18, 19, 309, 310.
Channel, **II**, 50, 239.
Charles VII (*king of France*), **II**, 75 (n. 82).
Charles the Bold (*duke of Burgundy*), **I**, 10; **II**, 65-67, 80, 82, 86, 87, 89, 92-94, 101, 105, 108, 109, 305, 335, 352, 357, 383, 419, 430.
Charles V (*emperor*), **I**, 35, 61, 75, 110, 111 (n. 13); **II**, 114 141, 147, 188, 200, 201, 213, 319 (n. 54), 352, 353, 362, 431.
Chavre (*Nicolas*), **II**, 29.
Cibrario, **I**, 119 (n. 27).
Claysson (*Edmond*), **II**, 146.
Clement V (*pope*), **II**, 352.
Cleve, **II**, 53 (n. 150), 103 (n. 87).
Clough (*Richard*), **I**, 59.

Coblence, **II**, 18.
Cocquel (merchant family), **II**, 226.
Coecke (Peter), **II**, 188.
Coignet (Michel), **II**, 349.
Cologne, **I**, 72-74, 75 (n. 55), 278, 288, 561; **II**, 19, 23, 25, 26, 39, 42, 47, 52-54, 74, 76, 82, 83 (n. 130), 104, 136, 149, 254, 260, 274, 309 (n. 4), 315, 373, 430.
Condé (prince of), **II**, 229.
Contarini (Alvise), **II**, 368 (n. 180).
Copenhagen, **II**, 79, 102, 165.
Coppenholle (Jan van), **II**, 97.

Cordoba, **I**, 217 (n. 3); **II**, 188.
Cornwall, **I**, 217 (n. 3).
Corsica, **II**, 213.
Courtrai, **II**, 15, 42, 46, 49, 89 (n. 2), 97, 110, 137, 145, 185, 186, 188, 190, 215, 229, 249, 252, 256, 258, 279, 324; **III**, 60, 61.
Coutereel (Pieter), **II**, 13.
Cracow, **I**, 60 (n. 178).
Curiël (Alonso de), **II**, 345.
Curtius (John), **II**, 262.
Cyprus, **II**, 423.

D

Daelman (Martin), **I**, 48 (n. 130).
Damme, **II**, 14, 50 (n. 128), 51, 56, 77 (n. 94), 78 (n. 101).
Danzig, **I**, 60, 228 (n. 6), 522, 523; **II**, 82, 102, 121, 128, 144, 146, 158, 159 (n. 106), 171, 216, 217, 223, 224, 226, 231, 232, 322, 340; **III**, 67.
Davidsone (Jan), **II**, 300 (n. 53).
De Bruyne (Daniël), **II**, 227, 337, 350, 365 (n. 163).
De Crayere (Philips), **I**, 46 (n. 121).
De Curiël (Alonso), see Curiël (Alonso de).
Deen (Aert), **II**, 343.
De Greve, **II**, 226.
De Hont (Cornelis), **I**, 30 (n. 71).
Deinze, **II**, 190.
Delft, **I**, 210, 228 (n. 2), 229; **II**, 122, 170.
Della Faille (merchant family), **I**, 36; **II**, 223, 224, 226, 257, 260 (n. 121), 270, 274, 278, 322, 323, 330 (n. 113), 338-340, 351.
De May (Nicolas), **II**, 110.
De Medaria (Peter), **II**, 330 (n. 112).

De (i) Medici, see *Medici family*.
Dendermonde, **I** 55, 233; **II**, 32 (n. 7), 47, 89 (n. 2), 170, 186; **III**, 60, 61.
Den Dungen, **I**, 229.
Denmark, **II**, 144, 158, 171, 201, 229, 231, 301.
De Pape (Frans), **I**, 229 (n. 14); **II**, 198 (n. 306), 300, 324, 335, 339.
De Reo (Nicolas), **II**, 350 (n.88).
De Ridder (Jan), **I**, 19 (n. 46), 21, 173.
De Schepper (Cornelis), **I**, 59.
Deurne, **I**, 52, 189; **II**, 248 (n. 22); **III**, 35.
Deux-Nèthes (department of), **I**, 69.
De Vries (Mathijs), **II**, 343 (n. 56).
De Vuyster (Theus), **I**, 46 (n. 121).
Diaz de Aguilla (Alonso), **II**, 240.
Diest, **I**, 12, 273, 547; **II**, 10, 54 (n. 154), 69, 71, 115, 188, 329.
Dijon, **I**, 43.
Dilbeek, **I**, 228.
Dinant, **II**, 119 (n. 29).
Dixmuide, **I**, 210; **II**, 137.

Dokkum, **II**, 141.
Dordrecht, **I**, 84, 99, 228 (n. 2), 262, 295; **II**, 14, 15, 19 (n. 96), 33, 40, 52, 53, 54 (n. 154), 161 (n. 114), 343.
Doria (*Andrea*), **II**, 111, 201, 213.
Dosovugo (*Thomas*), **II**, 343 (n. 56).
Douai, **II**, 121.
Dover (straits of), **II**, 229, 241.

Drente, **II**, 115.
Ducci (*Gaspar*), **II**, 202, 204, 355.
Duffel, **I**, 238 (n. 1), 477; **II**, 8, 10, 33, 118, 137, 175.
Du Mont (*Antoni*), **II**, 350 (n. 88).
Dunkirk, **II**, 252, 261, 262, 279.
Dutch, see Holland.
Duvel (*Hans*), **II**, 25 (n. 123).
Dyle, **I**, 69, 70, 98.

E

East-Indies, see India.
Edegem, **II**, 248 (n. 21); **III**, 35.
Edward IV (*king of England*), **II**, 83.
Edward VI (*king of England*), **II**, 213.
Eeklo, **I**, 55, 233; **II**, 80 (n. 118), 89 (n. 2), 190, 215, 229, 247, 256, 258; **III**, 60, 61.
Eersel, **III**, 36.
Egypt, **II**, 129.
Eindhout, **III**, 36.
Eke, **II** 118, 137, 175 (n. 177), 304.
Ekeren, **II**, 248 (n. 21); **III**, 35.
Elewijt, **I**, 517 (n. 1), 519.
Elizabeth I (*queen of England*), **I**, 55; **II**, 223, 228, 230, 237, 241, 242, 253, 264 (n. 155).
Emblehem, **III**, 36.
Emdem, **II**, 216, 229, 230, 237, 238, 253, 262, 317 (n. 45).
Enghien, **II**, 188, 323 (n. 79), 378 (n. 36).
England, **I**, 24 (n. 61), 44 (n. 116), 53-56, 79, 117 (n. 35), 152, 217 (n. 3), 273, 511 (n. 3); **II**, 7, 9-13, 15 (n. 68), 16-19, 21,22, 26, 27, 31, 34 (n. 19), 37-41, 43 (n. 78), 45-47, 49-56, 61 (n. 2), 62, 67-70, 73-75, 83,103, 105, 116 (n. 14), 119, 122, 123, 124 (n. 65), 133, 136, 141, 143-147, 162 (n. 116), 164-166, 177, 180-185, 187, 189, 191, 202, 204, 210, 213, 214, 218, 226, 228-230, 231 (n. 139), 236-238, 248, 253, 254, 257, 258, 262, 264(n. 155), 273, 274, 277, 278, 282, 290 (n. 6), 310, 313-315, 317, 318, 327, 329-331, 338, 339, 342, 345, 347, 352, 367, 368, 371-373, 378, 398, 399, 429-433; **III**, 60, 61.
Enkhuizen, **II**, 251.
Essen, **II**, 36.
Europe, passim.
Everaert (*Cornelis*) (*rhetorician*), **II**, 164.
Exeter, **I**, 72.

F

Far East, **II**, 124, 129, 177, 423.
Farnese (*Alexander*) (*duke of Parma*), **I**, 96, 173 (n. 1); **II**, 246, 248, 258-260, 265-267, 272, 274, 380, 417, 432.

Ferdinand of Aragon, **II**, 127, 149.
Flanders, passim.
Florence, **I**, 75; **II**, 20, 27, 50, 109-111, 140, 201, 348.
Florijszone (*Diric*), **II**, 342 (n. 54).

Flory (François), **II**, 331.

Flushing, **II**, 240, 241, 245, 250, 253, 263, 417, 424, 432.

Franc de Bruges, **II**, 15, 57 (n. 169).

France, **I**, 28, 32 (n. 82), 51, 56, 62, 83, 84, 95, 96, 109, 110, 113 (n. 21), 165, 287, 294, 295, 511 (n. 3), 515 (n. 9); **II**, 7, 12, 13, 24, 32, 40, 43, 63, 75, 78, 81 (n. 123), 83, 90, 95-97, 101, 114, 124, 126, 144, 145, 147, 148, 150, 154, 155, 160, 163, 171, 177, 182, 183, 187 (n. 248), 188, 189 (n. 260), 192, 201, 203, 209, 212-214, 221, 222, 224, 225, 228, 232, 237, 239, 242, 248, 257, 259, 261, 262, 264 (n. 155), 273, 277, 279, 281, 282, 299, 301 (n. 54), 306, 313, 314, 317, 320 (n. 58), 325(n. 88), 327, 331, 372 (n. 14), 392, 398, 422, 424, 434.

Francis I (king of France), **II**, 155.

G

Gascony, **II**, 75.

Geel, **I**, 273; **II**, 8, 10, 33, 69 (n. 46), 99, 245 (n. 2).

Geertruidenberg, **II**, 33.

Gelderland, **I**, 295; **II**, 13, 39, 92, 115, 129 (n. 94), 133, 141, 149, 159 (n. 106).

Geluveld, **II**, 269.

Gembloux, **II**, 69, 246.

Geneva, **II**, 44, 51, 59, 77, 83, 124, 314, 361, 430.

Genoa, **I**, 109 (n. 8); **II**, 20, 50, 104, 111, 150, 182, 188, 192, 201, 202, 205, 206, 213, 216, 217 (n. 51), 221, 222, 241, 242, 264, 273 (n. 21), 276 (n. 37), 280, 282, 320, 366, 367 (n. 175), 368; **III**, 76.

Georgstal (Thuringia), **I**, 522.

Frankfurt-am-Main, **I**, 60 (n. 178), 522; **II**, 11, 13, 24-26, 39, 44, 51-53, 54 (n. 153), 59, 74, 76, 82, 97, 98, 104, 124, 125, 128, 131, 136, 137, 217, 238, 256, 265 (n. 160), 315, 316, 321, 360, 367 (n. 177), 379 (n. 41), 429, 430.

French Flanders, **II**, 32 (n. 7), 120.

Frescobaldi (merchant family), **II**, 111, 131, 140.

Frisia, **I**, 210, 556; **II**, 47, 115, 122, 141, 170, 253, 301, 412.

Fris (Jan), **II**, 350 (n. 88).

Frits (Hans), **II**, 247 (n. 9).

Fuggerau (near Villach), **I**, 522.

Fugger (merchant family), **I**, 60, 522, 523; **II**, 122 (n. 48), 125-129, 131, 140, 147, 154, 158, 161, 205, 247, 252, 257, 320, 353 (n. 103), 367 (n. 177).

Funcus (Pierre), **II**, 350 (n. 88).

Furnes, **II**, 186.

Geraardsbergen, **II**, 188, 190, 323 (n. 79), 380.

Germany, **I**, 36, 111 (n. 17), 228, 278; **II**, 7, 11, 12, 19, 21-27, 32 (n. 8), 33, 39, 42, 47, 51-55, 63, 67, 69 (n. 46), 76, 82, 83, 97-100, 104, 105, 111, 114, 119, 120, 122-124, 126-133, 137, 140, 141, 143, 145, 146, 150, 156-161, 164, 166, 171, 177, 178, 181, 182, 185, 190, 192, 199, 200, 202, 204-206, 216-221, 223, 225, 229-231, 237, 238, 241, 245, 246, 262, 273, 278, 282, 290 (n. 6), 301 (n. 56), 309, 311-321, 325, 328, 331, 339, 363, 367 (n. 177), 373, 376 (n.29), 377, 407, 414-416, 423-425, 429-431, 433.

Gernaert (merchant), **II**, 226.

Gerona, **II**, 367 (n. 175).

Ghent, **I**, 85, 91, 96, 104 (n. 152), 233, 242, 295 (n. 2), 513 (n. 66), 553, 554, 559; **II**, 11, 12, 15, 24, 25, 38, 47-49, 52, 68 (n. 43), 70 (n. 57), 71 (n. 62), 77, 97, 98, 102, 110 (n. 128), 121, 151, 185, 188-190, 192, 219, 249, 255, 258, 279, 296 (n. 34), 298 (n. 45), 299, 307, 323 (n. 79),324, 369.

Gibraltar (straits of), **II**, 182, 257, 273, 318.

Gits, **II**, 269.

Gierle, **II**, 245 (n. 2).

Goa, **II**, 129.

Goes, **I**, 96, 288; **II**, 138, 300 (n. 53).

Goirle, **III**, 36.

Gomez (Ruy), **II**, 215.

Gorcum, **II**, 40.

Gouda, **I**, 229; **II**, 79 (n. 111), 102, 313 (n. 21).

H

Haarlem, **I**, 228, 229; **II**, 23, 31 (n. 3), 32, 54 (n. 154), 102, 190, 313 (n. 21).

Hagenbroek (hamlet of Lier), **I**, 238 (n. 1); **II**, 169, 174; **III**, 35.

Hainaut, **I**, 229, 233; **II**, 39, 57, 91, 92 (n. 19), 116, 170, 213, 220, 246, 250, 252, 257, 274, 277, 279, 307, 421 (n. 19).

Halen, **I**, 517 (n. 1), 547; **II**, 92.

Hallaar, **II**, 169; **III**, 35.

Halle, **II**, 248 (n. 21); **III**, 35.

Hamburg, **I**, 100, 119, 228, 522; **II**, 23, 79 (n. 111), 159 (n. 106), 216, 217, 222, 238, 253, 262, 273 (n. 24), 351, 367 (n. 175).

Hansa, **I**, 58, 300; **II**, 9, 12, 14, 15, 21, 24-27, 38-42, 45, 47, 50-54, 56,

Gramaye (Gerard), **I**, 262, 278, 295; **II**, 224, 226, 351 (n. 89), 366 (n. 171).

Granvelle (Nicolas Perrenot, lord of), **II**, 212, 233, 240.

Gravelines, **II**, 279.

's Gravenwezel, **II**, 248 (n. 21); **III**, 35.

Gresham (Thomas), **I**, 59; **II**, 238.

Groenberghe (Jacob), **II**, 179.

Groningen, **II**, 115, 122, 170, 301, 412.

Groot-Bijgaarden (Abbey of), **I**, 211, 218, 225, 229, 246, 249, 279, 288, 307.

Grote Waard, **II**, 33.

Gualterotti (merchant family), **II**, 111, 129, 131, 140.

Guicciardini (Luigi), **II**, 353, 368.

Guinea, **II**, 78.

Guydechon (Marc), **I**, 58; **II**, 57 (n. 170), 58.

63, 74, 75, 78 (n. 101), 79 (n. 111), 83, 103, 104, 108, 119-122, 157, 158, 164, 184 (n. 223), 218, 219, 224-226, 228, 237, 239, 251 (n. 51), 252-254, 274, 277, 313, 314, 321, 323, 326 (n. 91), 331, 338-340, 342, 345, 347, 373, 422, 429.

Hapert, **III**, 36.

Hapsburg, **I**, 110; **II**, 144, 146, 160, 171, 177, 180, 182, 201, 203, 206, 220, 398.

Haspengouw, **II**, 121, 171, 172, 176, 301, 302, 306.

Hasselt, **I**, 15 (n.42); **II**, 63 (n. 10), 99, 103 (n. 87).

Haug (merchant family), **II**, 353 (n. 103).

Hazebrouck, **II**, 258.

129

Heers (lord of), **II**, 10 (n. 27), 22, 298 (n. 43).

Heist-op-den-berg, **I**, 254, 273, 517 (n. 1); **II**, 169.

Hendrickx (Jan), **I**, 48 (n. 130), 49 (n. 130).

Henry VII (king of England), **II**, 123.

Henry VIII (king of England), **II**, 163, 184, 204, 373.

Henry III (king of France), **II**, 260 (n. 117).

Henry IV (king of France), **II**, 277.

Hensies, **I**, 229.

Herentals, **I**, 5, 8, 11, 12, 19 (n. 46), 23, 52, 55, 72 (n. 41), 84, 87, 91, 92 (n. 100), 93, 96-98, 101, 104, 105, 148, 179, 194, 218, 225, 269, 273, 279, 288, 295, 307, 517 (n. 1), 547; **II**, 10, 26 (n. 130), 68, 69, 80 (n. 118), 81 (n. 124), 86, 100, 110 (n. 128), 132 (n. 108), 136, 184, 190, 225, 226 (n. 100), 229, 262, 269, 270, 272 (n. 18), 315 (n. 34), 323, 329.

Herenthout, **I**, 11, 517 (n. 1); **II**, 245 (n. 2).

's-Hertogenbosch, **I**, 59, 229, 278, 510 (n. 1), 517 (n. 1), 546, 547; **II**, 31, 34, 37, 44, 49, 53 (n. 150), 69-71, 78, 92, 93, 98, 100, 107, 110 (n. 128), 113, 115, 116, 136, 137 (n. 135), 138, 151-153, 170, 175, 189 (n. 260), 190, 215, 225, 235, 255, 294 (n. 27), 355 (n. 117), 356.

Herve (Pays de), **II**, 170.

Herwaert (Christopher), **II**, 140.

Hesse, **II**, 128, 181, 328.

Heusden, **I**, 229; **II**, 116, 301.

Hochstetter (merchant family), **II**, 156, 200, 320.

Hoegaarden, **I**, 229, 294; **II**, 64, 172.

Hoeken, **II**, 40.

Hageloon, **III**, 36.

Hohenkirche, **I**, 522.

Holland, **I**, 56, 78, 93, 95, 101, 210, 217, 224, 229, 287, 294, 295, 511 (n. 3), 552, 557; **II**, 13, 16, 21-24, 27, 32-34, 38-41, 45-47, 53, 54, 56, 63, 67-70, 74, 75, 79, 80, 89, 97, 102, 103, 107 (n. 115), 120-122, 136, 138, 141, 157, 158, 164, 165, 170, 173, 179, 182-184, 190, 203, 218, 237, 240, 250, 251, 253, 255, 260 (n. 121), 273, 274, 277, 278, 282, 301, 313 (n. 21), 318, 327, 342, 345, 373, 412, 415, 417, 429.

Holstein, **II**, 115, 301, 412.

Hondschoote, **I**, 54; **II**, 33 (n. 9), 41, 42, 50 (n. 124), 77, 96, 101 (n. 73), 118, 138, 145, 175, 181, 186, 212, 215, 225, 229, 237, 240, 247, 252, 256, 258, 280, 317 (n. 46), 323, 377 (n. 32), 380, 398, 399; **III**, 60, 61, 106.

Honte, **I**, 510, 514 (n. 8); **II**, 33, 54, 96.

Hontenisse, **I**, 257.

Hooftman (Gillis), **II**, 226.

Hoogstraten, **I**, 5, 72 (n. 41), 96, 97, 148, 199, 234, 279, 288, 307; **II**, 8, 10, 33, 147, 173 (n. 167), 250, 269.

Hoogstraten (stadholder, count of), **II**, 147, 165, 179 (n. 195).

Hoorn, **I**, 169; **II**, 99, 137, 175, 258, 259, 274.

Hoorn (count of), **II**, 235.

Hormuz, **II**, 129.

Hove, **II**, 248 (n. 21); **III**, 35.

Hulst, **I**, 96, 102, 233, 288; **II**, 138.

Hungary, **I**, 60, 522, 523; **II**, 82, 123, 125, 126, 128, 130, 144, 145, 149, 154, 318, 320 (n. 56); **III**, 66.

Huy, **II**, 119 (n. 29).

Huybergen, **III**, 36.

I

Iberian Peninsula, I, 287; II, 78 (n. 100), 125, 137 (n. 138), 179, 180, 182, 221 (n. 74), 223, 239, 257, 260.

Ietegem, I, 517 (n. 1); II, 245 (n. 2).

Imhof (merchant family), II, 128, 131, 146 (n. 15), 353 (n. 102).

India, II, 124-127, 156, 273, 364, 424.

Italy, I, 62, 217 (n. 3); II, 9, 11, 12, 16-19, 20 (n. 102), 21, 23, 49-51, 56-58, 76, 77, 82, 83, 87, 103, 111, 119, 122, 124, 127, 129-131, 137 (n. 138), 144, 145, 149, 150, 154, 156, 159 (n. 106), 177, 179 (n. 198), 180-182, 186, 188, 190, 192, 201, 206, 213 (n. 18), 217, 220, 223, 224, 256, 259, 264 (n. 155), 265, (n. 160), 273, 280, 281, 282, 311, 312, 314, 319, 321, 325, 328, 331, 337-341, 343 (n. 60), 349, 353, 370, 372 (n. 14), 375, 416, 431.

Izegem, II, 190.

J

Jan-Baptist (Franciscan), II, 353.

Janssone (Harman), I, 21, 35, 85, 229, 249; II, 223, 224, 322, 323, 337, 339.

Joan (duchess of Brabant), II, 9, 26, 28, 29.

John III (duke of Brabant), II, 9, 369, 372.

John IV (duke of Brabant), II, 33, 39.

John the Fearless(duke of Burgundy), II, 28 (n. 148), 29, 57.

John of Bavaria, II, 40.

Jongelink (Nicolas), II, 351 (n. 89).

Juan (Don), II, 265 (n. 160).

K

Kallebeek, I, 257; II, 138, 319 (n. 54).

Kalmthout, I, 517 (n. 1), 519; III, 36.

Kapellen, I, 517 (n. 1).

Kelmis (Ida of), II, 126.

Kemmel, II, 118, 137.

Kempen, I, 11, 52, 79, 194, 210, 254, 273; II, 31, 34, 63, 89, 116, 138, 248, 269, 296 (n. 34), 298, 301, 372 (n. 13).

Kessel, I, 238 (n. 1); II, 168; III, 35.

Kiel, II, 253.

Kitson (English merchant), II, 338, 339.

Kleberg (Hans), II, 204.

Kock (Hans), II, 348 (n. 78).

Koningshooikt, I, 477; II, 170; III, 35.

Kortrijk (see Courtrai), I, 54, 233.

Kranz (Matthew), II, 126.

Kuik, I 229.

L

Lachenen (hamlet of Lier), I, 238 (n. 1).

Lamberti (Lamberto), II, 259.

Landen, I, 547; II, 69.

Land van Waas, see Waasland.

Langdorp, I, 295; II, 64.

Langemark, II, 42, 46, 49.

Languedoc, II, 11.

Laredo, **II**, 241.

La Rochelle, **II**, 224.

Le Havre, **II**, 229.

Leicester (earl of), **II**, 250, 260.

Leiden, **I**, 54; **II**, 13, 16, 38, 40, 41 (n. 60), 49 (n. 121), 53 (n. 154), 67-69, 79 (n. 111), 80, 89, 136, 145, 146, 164, 179 (n. 195), 185, 187, 262, 338, 342 (n. 54), 373, 379 (n. 40); **III**, 60, 61.

Leipzig, **I**, 60 (n. 178), 522; **II**, 125, 315.

Lejeune (Richard), **II**, 57 (n. 168).

Le Roy (Jaques), **II**, 57 (n. 168).

Levant, **II**, 154, 155, 177, 180, 182, 186, 190, 273, 311-313, 317, 318, 423.

Lichtaart, **II**, 245 (n. 2).

Liefkenshoek, **II**, 274.

Liège, **I**, 15 (n. 42), 24 (n. 61), 51, 551, 555, 561; **II**, 22, 39, 121 (n. 41), 147 (n. 30), 153 (n. 62), 189, 191, 262, 318 (n. 50), 319 (n. 54), 343 (n. 57), 402 (n. 35).

Lier, passim.

Lille, **I**, 242, 269; **II**, 71 (n. 62), 110 (n. 128), 137, 138, 185-187, 214, 245 (n. 2), 252, 279, 303, 324, 338.

Lillo, **I**, 477, 478-482, 552; **II**, 272 (n.18), 274.

Limburg, **I**, 554; **II**, 26, 99, 246, 274 (n. 31).

Lisbon, **I**, 288; **II**, 127, 129, 132 (n. 109), 155, 156, 159, 160, 177, 221 (n. 74), 281.

Livorno **II**, 182, 217 (n. 51), 273.

Lo, **II**, 186.

Lombardy, **II**, 22 (n. 109), 46, 47, 310, 314.

Lomellini (merchant family), **II**, 110.

London, **I**, 54, 56, 59, 62, 70; **II**, 52, 184, 186, 222, 228, 238, 326, 339, 351, 359 (n. 136); **III**, 76, 79, 107.

Loon op Zand, **III**, 36.

Lorenzo Chiarini (Giorgio di), **I**, 75.

Lorraine, **II**, 76, 136.

Louis de Male, **II**, 11, 12, 20, 22 (n. 109), 429.

Louis of Bavaria, **I**, 109.

Louis XI (king of France), **II**, 77 (n. 95), 79 (n. 114), 83, 84 (n. 141), 96.

Louis XII (king of France), **II**, 127, 140.

Louvain, **I**, 5, 23, 66 (n. 6), 73, 123, 229, 269, 294, 295, 517 (n. 1), 518, 546, 547, 559; **II**, 7, 10, 13, 17-19, 21 (n. 105), 28 (n. 146), 32 (n. 7), 35, (n. 21), 48, 64, 69-71, 80 (n. 118), 93, 99, 103 (n. 87), 107, 110 (n. 128), 113 (n. 4), 137 (n. 135), 138, 151, 152, 162 (n. 122), 172, 175, 195 (n. 293), 262, 294, 336, 353, 355 (n. 117), 356, 369, 372 (n. 13), 379 (n. 41), 395 (n. 20); **III**, 36.

Low Countries, passim.

Lübeck, **II**, 23, 38, 40, 50, 82, 104, 128 (n. 86), 158, 165, 183, 219, 229 (n. 126), 313, 317 (n. 46), 340, 348 (n. 78).

Lucca, **I**, 58; **II**, 28, 57 (n.168), 58, 111.

Ludingkhusen (Peter), **II**, 348 (n. 78).

Luithagen, **I**, 58 (n. 166).

Lüneburg, **I**, 522.

Luxemburg, **II**, 39, 57, 213.

Lyons, **I**, 109 (n. 8); **II**, 77 (n. 95), 83, 111 (n. 133), 124, 129, 141, 144, 154, 155, 180, 183, 201-204, 205 (n. 361), 221, 222, 255, 264, 265 (n. 161), 266 (n. 171), 280, 314, 348, 353 (n. 103), 355, 363, 366, 368, 430; **III**, 79.

Lys, **I**, 54; **II**, 170, 370.

M

Maaseik, I, 269; II, 69 (n. 46), 99, 137.

Maastricht, I, 15 (n. 42); II, 69, 126, 235.

Madeira, I, 306; II, 130, 423.

Madrid, II, 221, 222, 282.

Mainz, II, 54 (n. 153).

Malacca, II, 129.

Malestroit (*lord of*), I, 116, 121, 122.

Malines, passim.

Malta, II, 424.

Malynes (*Gerard de*), II, 351.

Manlich (*merchant family*), II, 156.

Mannini (*Salvestro e fratelli*), II, 16, 27.

Manting (*merchant family*), II, 321 (n. 60).

Maranos, II, 202.

Margaret of Austria, II, 119.

Margaret of Parma, II, 228, 230, 235.

Marnix van St. Aldegonde, I, 37; II, 260.

Marseilles, II, 129, 155, 182.

Mary of Burgundy, II, 67, 94, 109, 110, 335, 357.

Mary of Hungary, II, 162.

Mas (*Jan*), 350 (n. 88).

Massenhoven, II, 245 (n. 2), 272 (n. 18).

Maurice of Saxony, II, 213.

Maximilian of Austria, I, 110, 217; II, 89, 92 (n. 19), 95-97, 101, 103, 105, 109-111, 127, 141, 357.

Medici family (*dei*), II, 87, 110, 202, 361 (n. 140).

Medina del Campo, II, 201, 207, 221 (n. 74), 263, 265.

Mediterranean, II, 127, 130, 179, 223, 263, 273, 311 (n. 14), 314, 423, 433.

Mediterranean islands, II, 77, 105.

Meerbeek, I, 273.

Meerhout, I, 273; III, 36.

Memmingen, II, 54 (n. 153).

Menin, II, 132 (n. 109), 137, 186, 190, 247 (n. 11).

Mennens, II, 226.

Mennher, II, 350.

Merchtem, II, 10, 33.

Merksem, II, 248 (n. 21), 249; III, 35.

Metz, II, 213,

Meuse, I, 533; II, 213.

Meuse-region, II, 99, 118, 167.

Meussone (*Adriaen*), I, 80.

Middelburg, I, 96, 295; II, 13, 27, 79, 103, 121, 123, 183, 259, 262, 294 (n. 34), 367 (n. 175).

Middle East, II, 124, 127.

Mierlo, III, 36.

Mijle (hamlet of Lier), I, 238 (n. 1).

Milan, II, 129 (n. 93), 343 (n. 56), 367 (n. 175).

Millegem, I, 273.

Mol, I, 11-13, 17, 23, 179; II, 8, 10, 114, 171, 317 (n. 46), 372 (n. 13); III, 36, 47, 51.

Mons, I, 229; II, 116, 170, 186, 301, 303, 317 (n. 46).

Montils-les-Tours, II, 97.

Mookerheide, II, 245.

Mor (*Pierre*), II, 350 (n. 88).

Morillon (*bishop*), II, 240.

Moresnet, II, 126.

Morkhoven, II, 245 (n. 2).

Mortsel, II, 248 (n. 21); III, 35.

Mühlberg, II, 213.

Munich, I, 116 (n. 30), 159.

N

Naarden. **II**, 67, 89.
Namur, **I**, 15 (n. 42), 18 (n. 42), 550, 556; **II**, 110 (n. 128), 119 (n. 29), 121 (n. 41).
Nancy, **II**, 89, 92, 105.
Nantes, **II**, 252.
Naples, **II**, 147, 182, 257, 273.
Narva, **II**, 217, 224, 229, 340.
Netherlands, passim.
Neuféglise, see Nieuwkerke.
Neusohl, **I**, 522.
Neuss, **II**, 53 (n. 150).
New Town (of Antwerp), **I**, 521; **II**, 189, 193.
New World, see America.
Nieppe, **II**, 137.

Nieuwkerke, **I**, 54, 55, 477, 529-531; **II**, 104, 118, 137, 145, 164 (n. 131), 175, 185-187, 258, 323, 329.
Nieuwpoort, **II**, 110 (n. 128), 252, 279.
Nijlen, **I**, 238 (n. 1); **III**, 35, 36.
Nijmegen, **II**, 53 (n. 150), 253.
Nivelles, **I**, 517 (n. 1); **II**, 86.
Normandy, **I**, 273; **II**, 40, 41, 115 (n. 12), 183, 224, 262, 301.
North Sea, **I**, 557; **II**, 74, 119, 144, 145, 156, 217, 223, 239, 433.
Nuremberg, **I**, 60 (n. 178), 522; **II**, 24, 25 (n. 123), 39, 51, 52, 54 (n. 153), 58, 82, 124, 125, 128, 159 (n. 106), 367 (n. 175).
Nutin (Jehan), **II**, 110.

O

Oelegem, **III**, 36.
Oevel, **III**, 36.
Onze-Lieve-Vrouw-Waver, **I**, 63, 150, 507, 509; **II**, 66 (n. 26), 173 (n. 167), 175 (n. 175), 307.
Op te Locht (near St. Lenaarts), **I**, 517 (n. 1).

Ostend, **II**, 277.
Oudburg (Castellany of the), **II**, 307.
Outre-Meuse, **II**, 115, 301, 412.
Ouwen (near Herentals), **I**, 517 (n. 1), 518.
Overijsel, **II**, 115, 122, 149, 301, 412.

P

Palermo, **II**, 367 (n. 175).
Pardo, **II**, 345.
Paris, **I**, 6 (n. 8), 69, 73, 108, 139 (n. 6), 143 (n. 13); **II**, 57, 221, 222, 240, 265 (n. 160), 337 (n. 21), 353.
Park (Abbey of), **II**, 296 (n. 34), 361 (n. 140), 372 (n. 13).
Parma, see *Farnese (Alexander)*.
Parma, **I**, 217 (n. 3).
Passau, **II**, 213.

Passendaele, **II**, 269.
Pavia, **II**, 149.
Pérez de Varrón (Martin), **II**, 276 (n. 39).
Perez (Loeys), **II**, 348 (n. 78).
Peri Gio (Domenico), **II**, 276 (n. 37).
Perre (Gommaer), **I**, 40 (n. 107).
Peru, **II**, 192.
Philip the Bold (duke of Burgundy), **II**, 15, 26, 28, 29, 107.

Philip the Good (*duke of Burgundy*), **I**, 8 (n. 20), 57, 108; **II**, 34 (n. 19), 36, 48, 56-58, 62, 67, 76, 78, 80, 84-86, 92, 94, 107, 335, 336, 361, 362, 382, 396 (n. 22), 409.

Philip the Fair (*duke of Burgundy, king of Spain*), **I**, 59 (n. 175), 68; **II**, 98, 114, 119, 120, 123, 383.

Philip II (*king of Spain*), **I**, 61; **II**, 193, 206, 214, 221, 223, 233, 237, 261, 264, 276, 280, 362, 365, 416.

Philip of Cleve, **II**, 97, 98, 100, 103.

Philippine, **II**, 274.

Philips (*merchant*), **II**, 226.

Picardy **I**, 24 (n. 61); **II**, 32, 57, 101, 120, 122 (n. 51), 301, 304 (n. 72).

Pinne (*Peter*), **I**, 45.

Pius V (*pope*), **II**, 353 (n. 103).

Placenza, **I**, 109 (n. 8).

Plantin (*Christopher*), **I**, 36, 48, 49 (n. 133), 249; **II**, 189, 378.

Poederlee, **II**, 245 (n. 2).

Poland, **II**, 11, 24 (n. 116), 32 (n. 8), 74, 82, 123, 229, 232, 302.

Polders, **II**, 167.

Pommeroeuil, **I**, 229.

Poperinge, **II**, 118, 137, 164, 175, 184, 186, 187, 258, 323, 338.

Poppel, **I**, 517 (n. 1).

Portinari (*Tomaso*), **II**, 110.

Portugal, **I**, 96, 287, 288, 306, 307; **II**, 77, 78, 103, 105, 120 (n. 30), 123-131, 143, 144, 153-157, 159, 161, 177, 178 (n. 191), 179, 191, 192, 199, 202, 203, 205, 217(n. 51), 237, 250, 253-256, 263, 273, 274, 277, 280-282, 317, 362, 363, 415, 423, 424, 431.

Postel (Abbey of), **II**, 296 (n. 34), 298 (n. 43), 361 (n. 140), 372 (n. 13).

Pot (*Peter*), **II**, 58.

Prato (*Francisco de*), **II**, 343 (n. 60).

Prussia, **II**, 11, 24 (n. 116), 32 (n. 8), 39, 40, 74, 78 (n. 101), 158, 232, 313.

Pruynen (*Aert*), **II**, 126, 130.

Pruynen (*Christopher*), **II**, 224, 226.

Pruystinck (*Elooi*), **II**, 153.

Putte (near Kapellen), **I**, 517 (n. 1).

Q

Quiévrain, **I**, 229.

Quirini, **II**, 119 (n. 29).

R

Rapondi (*Dino*), **II**, 29, 57 (n. 168).

Ravels, **III**, 36.

Reali (*merchant family*), **II**, 110.

Reimerswaal, **I**, 96, 288; **II**, 138.

Rem brothers (*merchants*), **II**, 146 (n. 15).

Requesens y Zuniga (*Don Luis de*), **II**, 245, 253, 254, 432.

Reval, **II**, 122 (n. 50), 217, 317 (n. 46).

Rhesen (*merchant family*), **II**, 146.

Rhine, **I**, 30 (n. 73), 72, 73, 83, 84, 110, 278, 295, 561; **II**, 39, 52, 53 (n. 150), 54 (n. 153), 63, 161 (n. 114), 183, 320 (n. 58), 395, 398, 424.

Rhineland, **II**, 76, 373.
Ricard (*J.P.*), **I**, 86, 88, 92, 96, 98.
Riga, **II**, 217, 322 (n. 74), 340.
Rioseco, **II**, 221, 237.
Roda (*Jeronimo de*), **II**, 254, 343 (n. 56).
Roermond, **II**, 251.
Roeselare, **I**, 233; **II**, 190, 269.
Roeulx, **I**, 229.
Rome, **II**, 149, 150, 361 (n. 140), 367 (n. 175).
Rosebeke, **II**, 269.

Rott (*Konrad*), **II**, 257, 266.
Rotterdam, **I**, 257; **II**, 262.
Rouen, **I**, 104 (n. 152);**II**, 222, 224, 235, 240, 252, 262, 265 (n. 160), 326.
Ruiz (*merchant family*), **I**, 62, 121, 525; **II**, 266 (n. 171), 325 (n. 88), 348, 353 (n. 103).
Rupel, **I**, 257.
Rupelmonde, **I**, 257 (n. 3), 262.
Rupprecht (*Palatine count*), **II**, 129 (n. 94).
Russia, **I**, 155; **II**, 160 (n. 111).

S

Saintonge, **I**, 287.
Sambre, **II**, 213.
Sandow, **II**, 122 (n. 50).
Sanguin (*Guillaume*), **II**, 57 (n. 168).
Saône, **II**, 129, 154.
Sâo Tomé, **I**, 306; **II**, 179, 423.
Saragossa, **II**, 188.
Savonne (*Pierre*), **II**, 331.
Scandinavia, **II**, 327.
Scania, **I**, 101, 277, 278; **II**, 43, 78, 422.
Scheldt, **I**, 57, 59, 510, 511 (n. 3), 514 (n. 8), 551, 553-562; **II**, 33, 54, 97, 101, 103, 144, 154, 177, 231, 251, 253, 255, 257, 259, 260, 265, 273, 360, 417, 428.
Schelle, **I**, 517 (n. 1).
Schets (*merchant family*), **II**, 126, 130, 217 (n. 51), 345.
Schiedam, **II**, 67.
Schijndel, **I**, 229; **II**, 116, 301.
Schoten, **I**, 63, 150, 507, 509; **II**, 173 (n. 167), 175 (n. 175), 307.
Scotland, **II**, 27, 144.
Seine, **II**, 40.
Serbia, **II**, 311.

Setubal, **I**, 288.
Seville, **I**, 35, 56; **II**, 159, 179, 180, 188, 205, 206, 215, 221-224, 237, 241,263,281,282,322,326,363;**III**, 79.
Sicily, **II**, 423.
Siena, **II**, 213.
Schleswig, **II**, 115, 301, 412.
Sluis, **II**, 76, 77 (n. 94), 78, 98, 103, 110 (n. 128), 253, 279.
Smeekaert (*Willem*), **I**, 40 (n. 108).
Soert (hamlet of Lier), **I**, 238 (n. 1).
Soignes (forest of), **I**, 254.
Soignies, **I**, 562.
Sokotora, **II**, 129.
Soliman II (*sultan*), **II**, 155.
Somme area, **II**, 61 (n. 2), 301.
Sound, **II**, 102, 114, 122, 157, 158, 164, 165, 251, 413.
Spain, **I**, 24 (n. 61), 56, 58, 62, 65, 79, 165 (n. 75), 287, 295, 526; **II**, 67, 77, 103, 105, 110, 119, 122, 124, 125, 129-131, 136, 144, 146, 147, 159, 177-180, 183 (n. 219), 187, 188, 189 (n. 260), 190-192, 201, 202, 205, 206, 209, 211, 214-217,

221-224, 235-237, 240-246, 251, 253, 254, 256, 259, 260, 263-265, 267, 269, 273 (n. 21), 274, 277, 280-282, 317, 318, 320, 325 (n. 88), 327, 330, (n. 112), 338, 341, 343 (n. 60), 353, 354, 366, 372, 378, 415, 416, 423, 431.

Speyer, II, 171, 218, 431.

Spinelli (*merchant family*), II, 361 (n. 140).

Staden, II, 269.

St. Antonius-Brecht, II, 248 (n. 21); III, 35.

St. Bavo (Abbey of), II, 296 (n. 34).

St. Bernard (Abbey of), II, 319 (n. 54).

Steenbergen, I, 95, 97, 101, 102, 547; II, 43 (n. 78), 62, 78 (n. 104), 337.

Steenvoorde, II, 234.

Stekene, I, 257.

Stettin-am-Oder, I, 522, 523; II, 121, 128, 144; III, 67.

St. Lenaarts-Brecht, I, 517 (n. 1), 519.

St. Malo, II, 224, 240, 252, 322.

St. Michiel (Abbey of), II, 361 (n. 140).

St. Michielsgestel, I, 229.

St. Omer, II, 231.

Strasbourg, II, 39, 149.

Stryt (*Willem*), I, 23 (n. 61).

St. Truiden (St. Trond), I, 15 (n. 42); II, 22 (n. 113), 71, 100 (n. 69), 188, 330.

Sudan, II, 177.

Suderman (*Doctor*), II, 218.

Swabia, II, 77.

Sweden, II, 224, 229, 231.

Switzerland, II, 17.

Syria, II, 423.

T

Ter Doest (Abbey of), II, 247 (n. 13).

Ter Duinen (Abbey of), II, 296 (n. 34).

Teteringen, III, 36.

The Hague, II, 67, 89.

Thomas Aquinas, I, 39.

Thuringia, I, 522.

Thurzo (*merchant and engineer*), I, 60, 522.

Tielen, II, 245 (n. 2).

Tienen, I, 59, 217 (n. 3), 517 (n. 1), 547, 562; II, 21 (n. 105), 32 (n. 7), 69, 71, 93, 110 (n. 128), 137 (n. 135), 172; III, 36.

Tielt, II, 190, 298 (n. 45).

Tilburg, III, 36.

Toledo, II, 188.

Tongerlo (Abbey of), I, 52, 277 (n. 1), 507, 508; II, 8, 34, 62 (n. 5), 63 (n. 10), 92, 115, 175, 210, 211, 245 (n. 2), 248, 296 (n. 34), 297, 298, 361 (n. 140), 372 (n. 13); III, 36, 37.

Tongres, I, 15 (n. 42).

Toul, II, 213.

Tourcoing, II, 164, 184, 323, 338.

Tournai, I, 262; II, 13, 144, 186, 188, 232, 234, 258, 303.

Tournon (*cardinal de*), II, 201.

Treves, II, 335.

Triest, I, 523; III, 67.

Troyes, I, 68, 72-74, 75 (n. 55).

Tucher (*merchant family*), I, 525; II, 146, 156.

Tunis. II, 201.

Turkey, II, 111, 155, 180, 201, 213, 221, 223, 257.

Turnhout, I, 257, 477, 517 (n. 1),

518; **II**, 8, 10, 26 (n. 130), 63
(n. 10), 118, 138, 175, 190, 259,

262, 329, 377 (n. 32).
Tyrol, **II**, 130 (n. 98).

U

Udenhout, **III**, 36.
Uilenberg (near Herenthout), **I**, 517
(n. 1), 518.

Ulm, **II**, 54 (n. 153).
Utrecht, **II**, 24, 34, 40, 74, 75, 235,
343.

V

Valenciennes, **II**, 186, 188, 232, 235,
303.
Valkenburg, **II**, 26.
Valois, **II**, 101, 120.
Van Beeringen (*Jan*), **I**, 48 (n. 129).
Van Bell (*Jaspar*), **II**, 223 (n. 85),
323, 349 (n. 78).
Van Bombergen (*merchant family*),
II, 344.
Van Buyten (*Peter*), **II**, 348 (n. 78).
Van Dale (*Paul*), **II**, 179, 231.
Van den Blocke (*Jacob*), **II**, 357.
Van den Bossche (*Bernaert*), **I**, 49
(n. 131).
Van der Molen (*merchant family*), **I**,
35; **II**, 323, 337, 338, 359.
Van der Sickele (*Simon*), **II**, 26.
Van Eemeren, **II**, 343 (n. 56).
Van Gistel (*Gerard*), **II**, 132 (n. 109).
Van Houtte (*Joos*), **I**, 48 (n. 129).
Van Immerseel (*Elisabeth*), **I**, 6.
Van Immerseel (*merchant family*),
II, 274, 340.
Van Lare (*François*), 365 (n. 163).
Van Lendrichusen (*Johann*), **II**, 54
(n. 153).
Van Liebergen, **II**, 226.
Van Mijnden (*Thomas*), **II**, 324
(n. 81).
Van Olen (*Simon*), **I**, 45.

Van Rechtergem (*Nicholas*), **II**, 126,
130, 140.
Van Rossum (*Maarten*), **II**, 159
(n. 106), 164, 167, 173, 193, 413,
415 (n. 10).
Van Schelle (*Claus*), **I**, 48 (n. 129).
Van Schoonbeke (*Gillebert*), **I**, 76
(n. 59), 262, 294 (n. 9); **II**, 189,
193, 319 (n. 54).
Vaucelles, **II**, 213, 214.
Vaughan (*English merchant*), **II**, 204.
Veere, **II**, 121.
Veerle, **III**, 36.
Venezuela, **II**, 129.
Venice, **I**, 75, 306, 323; **II**, 20, 50,76,
82, 103, 104, 119 (n. 29), 124-130,
141, 153-157, 180, 188, 257, 313,
320 (n. 56), 341 (n. 50), 367
(n.175), 368 (n. 180); **III**, 67, 76,
79.
Verbrugge (*Joos*), **I**, 46 (n. 121).
Verdun, **II**, 213.
Vienna, **I**, 60 (n. 178); **II**, 123 (n. 58).
Viersel, **III**, 36.
Villach, **I**, 522; **II**, 205.
Villalon, **II**, 202, 352.
Villalon, **II**, 221, 237.
Villers, **I**, 517 (n. 1), **II**, 296 (n. 34).
Vilvoorde, **I**, 123; **II**, 32 (n. 6), 69,
151.
Visé, **I**, 262.

Vleminckx (*Jan*), **II**, 126, 130.
Vlijmen, **I**, 229.

Voorschoten, **II**, 272 (n. 18).
Vorselaar, **II**, 245 (n. 2).

W

Waalwijk, **I**, 229.
Waasland, **I**, 223, 257, 556, 557; **II**, 170.
Walcheren, **I**, 56, 295, 553; **II**, 55, 77, 79, 80, 121, 136, 156, 157, 237, 239, 330.
Walem, **II**, 8, 10, 33,
Walloon provinces, **II**, 248.
Washington (*Thomas*), **II**, 344.
Webbecom (*Jan*), **II**, 351 (n. 89).
Wechelderzande, **II**, 245 (n. 2).
Weddington (*John*), **II**, 331 (n. 119), 338 (n. 29), 342, 347.
Weert, **I**, 54, 139, 269, 560; **II**, 42, 69 (n. 46), 99, 134, 137, 162, 175, 194, 229, 239, 258, 259, 274, 323, 329, 397, 422; **III**, 43, 47, 48, 52, 55, 59, 90, 103, 118.
Weelde, **I**, 517 (n. 1).
Welser (*merchant family*), **II**, 128, 129, 131, 156, 161, 257, 349 (n. 85).
Wenceslas (*duke of Brabant*), **I**, 228; **II**, 9, 29.

Wervik, **I**, 54; **II**, 42, 46, 49, 186, 187, 188, 323 (n. 80).
West African coast **II**, 77, 78, 105, 125, 126.
Westdeurne (near Wuustwezel), **I**, 517, (n. 1).
Westerhoven, **III**, 36.
Westerlo, **II**, 245 (n. 2).
West-Indies, **II**, 216, 223, 273, 364, 412, 415, 416, 417, 424.
Westmalle, **I**, 254, 517 (n. 1), 518.
Westphalia, **II**, 15, (n. 68), 126.
Wiekevorst, **III**, 36.
Wielingen, **II**, 33, 54, 56.
William of Orange, **II**, 235, 236, 251, 253, 254.
William I (*king of the Netherlands*), **I**, 70.
Winchester, **I**, 65.
Wommelgem, **II**, 248 (n. 21); **III**, 35.
Würzburg, **II**, 159.
Wuustwezel, **I**, 210, 517 (n. 1); **II**, 248 (n. 21); **III**, 35.

Y

Ympyn (*Jan*), **II**, 331.
Ypres, **I**, 477; **II**, 11, 15, 24, 48, 104, 118 (n. 22), 137, 164 (n. 131), 185,
186, 247 (n. 11), 249, 258, 269, 271, 303 (n. 68), 323, 329, 338, 369.

Z

Zandhoven, **II**, 272 (n. 18).
Zandvliet, **I**, 477, 478-482, 517 (n. 1), 559; **II**, 272 (n. 18).

Zeeland, **I**, 28, 57, 59, 65, 77, 79, 95, 96, 102, 189, 194, 233, 277 (n. 1), 278, 287-290, 511(n. 3), 550-552,

INDEX OF SUBJECTS

A

Aas, see Weights, **I**, 72-79.

Absolutism, **II**, 94.

Active trade, see Trade.

Adjustment, **I**, 151, 159, 173, 183, 510, 529.

Administration, **I**, 8 (n. 20), 13,15, 27, 37, 52, 58, 76; **II**, 44, 64 (n. 16), 70, 73, 233, 277-279, 282, 375, 421 (n. 19), 432.

Agio, **II**, 58, 147 (n. 30), 163 (n. 127), 233 (n. 151), 236 (n. 169), 259 (n. 107), 351.

Aids, **II**, 16, 28 (n. 146), 49, 58 (n. 173), 86, 107, 109, 147, 152, 162, 200, 203, 214, 271, 349 (n. 83), 354, 383.

Alum, **I**, 78; **II**, 46 (n. 94), 103, 319, 320.

Ame, see Measures of contents, **I**, 80-102.

Ammunition works, **I**, 189, 197, 262.

Anabaptism, **II**, 153, 194.

Anarchism, **II**, 153.

Anchorage, anchorage list, **I**, 56; **II**, 156, 237.

Annuity (see Rent), **I**, 34, 489-492; **II**, 58, 85, 87 96 (n. 38), 106, 107, 109, 139, 141, 146, 147, 149, 165, 174, 192, 206, 307, 336, 337, 354, 355, 364, 375, 402 (n. 33).

Anticlericalism, **II**, 152, 153, 212.

Apiculture, **II**, 63.

Apothecary, **I**, 78.

Appréciation, **I**, 7, 16, 17.

Apprentice, **I**, 46, 47, 55, 333, 529, 532; **II**, 42, 70, 81 (n. 121), 197, 215; **III**, 62.

Arable land, **II**, 8, 36, 61, 115, 150, 167, 171, 173, 295, 298, 301 (n. 56); **III**, 71.

Are, see Measures of length and area, **I**, 102-105.

Armament industry, **II**, 262.

Armistice, see Peace, see Truce.

Army, Mercenary army, **II**, 34 (n. 19), 87, 246, 248, 297.

Arrears, **I**, 488; **II**, 98 (n. 54), 107, 115, 117, 174, 247, 272.

Arts, **II**, 71, 188, 375.

Asientos, **I**, 35, 36, 61, 526; **II**, 147, 205, 213 (n. 18), 242, 256, 257, 265, 266, 276, 280, 281, 355, 364, 432.

Assignment, **II**, 29, 202, 206, 334, 335, 340-349, 350 (n. 88), 351, 358-360, 364, 367 (n. 178), 368, 434.

Aval, see Guarantee.

Avena sativa, see Oats.

Avena strigosa, see Rough oats.

Average method, **I**, 145-152, 163 (n. 65), 165, 166; **II**, 28, 29, 33; **III**, 14-119.

B

Baize, **II**, 186, 187.

Baker, **I**, 6, 7, 18, 19; **II**, 175 (n. 177), 324.

Balance of payment, **II**, 300 (n. 52), 415, 416.

Balance of trade, **I**, 119, 488, 493-496, 524 (n. 2); **II**, 191 (n. 269), 412, 415 (n. 13).

Ban, *bannum*, **I**, 66, 75.

Bank, banking technique, **II**, 76, 87, 108, 206 (n. 366), 355-360.

Bank, clearance bank, **II**, 107, 108, 341, 342, 355-358, 359 (n. 136), 367.

Bank, deposit bank, **II**, 105-109, 320, 341, 353 (n. 103), 355-357, 358, (n. 130), 359 (n. 136), 360, 364.

Bank, discount bank, **II**, 360, 434.

Bank, Exchange Bank of Amsterdam, **II**, 367.

Bank, issuing bank, **II**, 434.

Bank of England, **II**, 368.

Banker, see Merchant-banker.

Bankguilder of Amsterdam, *bank-gulden* of Amsterdam, see Money, **I**, 107-135.

Bankrupt, bankruptcy, **I**, 35, 526; **II**, 86, 105-110, 131, 146, 178, 200, 207, 214, 216, 220, 221, 223, 237, 241, 263, 270, 277, 282, 355, 357, 363, 364, 416.

Bankruptcy Court, **I**, 21, 36, 37, 121.

Bargaining power, **II**, 123, 134, 135, 194, 196-198, 387, 403, 432, 434, 435.

Barge, see Measures of contents, **I**, 80-102.

Bark, **I**, 29, 31 (n. 76), 100, 102, 242-244; **II**, 116, 118, 173, 299, 304 (n. 73); **III**, 22, 23.

Barley, **I**, 13, 21, 98, 189-193; **II**, 32, 298 (n. 41), 392, 393; **III**, 18, 19, 96.

Barrel, see Measures of contents, **I**, 80-102.

Barrel herring, **I**, 101, 277-282; **II**, 251; **III**, 22, 23.

Barrow man, **II**, 132.

Barter, **II**, 126, 334, 335, 338.

Basket, see Weights, **I**, 72-79, and Measures of contents, **I**, 80-102.

Beans, **I**, 98; **II**, 299.

Beef cattle, **I**, 508; **II**, 62, 175, 210.

Beehive, beekeeping, **I**, 508; **II**, 301.

Beer, **I**, 28, 30, 60, 61, 66, 80-83, 84 (n. 86), 91, 100, 145 (n. 18), 228, 294, 510, 520, 521, 534-537; **II**, 12, 15 (n. 66), 79 (n. 111), 86, 99 (n. 65), 152, 172, 249, 261 (n. 129), 276, 301, 313, 335; **III**, 64, 87.

Beer, Brabant beer, **II**, 120, 172.

Beer, Dutch beer, **I**, 229, 294; **II**, 20, 23, 24 (n. 116), 32, 79 (n. 111), 120, 313 (n. 20).

Beer, Eastern beer, North German beer, **I**, 228 (n. 6); **II**, 20, 23, 24 (n. 116), 32 (n. 8), 120, 313.

Beer, Haarlem beer, **II**, 24 (n. 116), 31 (n. 3), 32, 54 (n. 153), 102, 313 (n. 20).

Beer, Hamburg beer, **II**, 24 (n. 116), 79 (n. 111).

Beer, *knol* beer, **I**, 229.

Beer, *koyte* beer, **I**, 229; **II**, 79 (n. 111), 102.

Beer brewing industry, **I**, 91 (n. 97), 228, 229, 294 (n. 9); **II**, 24, 31, 32, 54 (n. 154), 99, 102, 189, 301, 302, 313, 393.

Begging, II, 64, 69, 193, 250.

Béguine, I, 41.

Bell-ringer, I, 39.

Betting, II, 202, 364, 365.

Beurse, see *Bourse*.

Bimetallic system, I, 111.

Birth, birth rate, II, 291, 405.

Black Death, II, 9.

Black oats, see Rough oats.

Bleacher, I, 333.

Bleaching industry, II, 190.

Blecker, see Wood gatherer.

Bodin effect, I, 116, 121, 122.

Bonds, bonds to bearer (see also Letter obligatory and Clause ,,payable to bearer"); II, 141,163, 202, 215, 263, 322, 323, 343 (n. 60), 344 (n. 61), 351 (n. 89), 355, 360, 361, 366 (n. 171), 367 (n. 178).

Book-keeper, I, 28, 72; II, 334.

Book-keeping, I, 25, 28, 60, 64, 109, 139 (n. 5), 141, 145, 488; II, 331, 338 (n. 29), 341, 342, 347, 350, 433.

Book transfer, II, 341, 342, 345, 348, 366-368.

Boot, see Measures of contents, I, 80-102.

Boscool, see Charcoal.

Bourgeoisie, I, 509; II, 55, 93, 94, 96.

Bourse (see also Exchange), II, 111, 233, 239, 330, 353, 366 (n. 168), 367, 368.

Bourse, English *Bourse*, English House, II, 329, 330.

Boxharing, see Smoked herring.

Brabant Fairs, passim.

Brand, see Herring.

Bread, I, 158, 159, 534-537; II, 17, 48, 114, 232, 390, 395; III, 14, 87.

Brewer, I, 30, 82, 189, 194, 228, 229 (n. 11); II, 24 (n. 116), 335.

Brewery, I, 21, 521; II, 31 (n. 3), 99 (n. 65), 193, 393 (n. 15).

Brewing industry, see Beer brewing industry.

Brick, brick making, I, 27, 94, 100, 144, 255-261; II, 81 (n. 123), 133(n. 118), 138, 146 (n. 14), 189, 227, 229, 319 (n. 54), 387 (n. 72), 397;III, 46-49, 54, 55, 103.

Brick maker, I, 94, 257; II, 319 (n. 54).

Broker, II, 126, 132, 192, 225 (n. 97), 279, 317 (n. 46), 358-360, 378.

Bronze, I, 67-69.

Buck-wheat, I, 98; II, 298 (n. 41).

Budget, I, 63, 155, 156, 158, 533-538; II, 84, 107, 263, 374, 385 (n. 63), 393 (n. 15), 395 (n. 19, 20), 396 (n. 21), 424.

Buideldrager, see Porter.

Building, building cycle, I, 44 (n. 116).

Building, building industry, building sector, I, 50, 149, 160, 533, 538, 539-544; II, 13, 17, 43, 44, 72, 81, 97, 98 (n. 54), 118, 133-135, 136 (n. 132), 145, 146 (n. 14), 162, 192, 193, 195, 197, 219, 227, 229, 230, 236, 239, 253, 258, 259, 276, 319 (n. 54), 379, 381 (n. 53), 385, 396 (n. 22), 397, 403, 405, 422; III, 71.

Bunder, see Measures of length and area, I, 102-105.

Burgundian guilder, see Money, I, 107-135.

Burler, II, 370 (n. 9).

Bushel, see Measures of contents, I, 80-102.

Butter, I, 27, 78, 144, 146-148, 158, 210-216, 287, 533, 535-537; II, 9, 101, 134, 150, 161, 173, 194, 197,

210, 212, 219, 251, 381 (n. 53), 385, 386, 390, 395, 409, 410, 413, 414, 416, 417; **III**, 46-49, 52-55, 90, 91, 99, 118.
Butter, Dixmuide butter, **I**, 210.
Butter, Dutch butter, **I**, 78, 210; **II**, 103, 122, 301.

Butter, Flemish butter, **I**, 78, 114, 210; **II**, 102, 103, 170, 301.
Butter, Frisian butter, **I**, 210.
Butter, Kempen butter, **I**, 210.
Button maker, **II**, 226.
Buytenbier, **II**, 99 (n. 65).
Buytenlaken, **I**, 269.

C

Calamine, **II**, 126.
Calories, **II**, 390, 395.
Calvinism, **II**, 212, 228, 232-236, 260, 432.
Cambios de feria a feria, see Deposit from fair to fair.
Cambium, see Exchange.
Canvas, **I**, 103, 273; **II**, 176, 183, 224, 318.
Candles, tallow candles, **I**, 27, 31 (n. 76), 79, 249-253; **III**, 22, 23.
Candles, wax candles, **I**, 79.
Cane sugar, see Sugar.
Capital, **I**, 120, 161; **II**, 21, 28, 29, 36, 57-59, 85, 131, 134 (n. 121), 146, 157, 160, 174, 179, 192, 199-201, 203, 204, 206, 218, 221, 239, 241-243, 256, 263, 265, 269-273, 307, 311, 316, 319, 320, 322, 323, 335, 339, 353 (n. 103), 361-363, 371, 374, 375, 401, 412, 414-416, 431, 434.
Capitalism, capitalistic organization, **II**, 189, 191, 317-321, 325 (n. 88), 380, 381, 386, 419-425, 435.
Carder, **II**, 118.
Carolus guilder, see Money, **I**, 107-135.
Carpenter, **I**, 40, 45, 46, 333 (n. 2), 350-365, 407-420, 441-444, 457-469, 504 (n. 8); **II**, 134, 135

(n. 126), 175 (n. 177), 193, 195, 227 (n. 115), 259, 275, 279 (n. 58), 304.
Carpet, carpet weaving, **II**, 188, 380.
Cart, see Measures of contents, **I**, 80-102.
Casa da India, **II**, 129.
Cashier, **II**, 359, 360.
Catholicism, **II**, 235.
Cattle, cattle breeding, cattle raising, **I**, 28, 52, 91 (n. 97), 145 (n. 19); **II**, 8, 31, 34, 62, 92, 93, 114, 115, 117, 122, 168, 170, 173, 174, 210, 211, 246, 248, 269, 270 (n. 3), 293, 298, 301, 396, 410, 413; **III**, 37.
Cattle, cattle fodder, **II**, 116, 168, 298.
Cattle, cattle market, **I**, 59 (n. 176); **II**, 251, 255, 301, 395.
Cattle, cattle plague, **II**, 62 (n. 5), 115 (n. 11).
Census, **II**, 35 (n. 22), 37, 90, 139 (n. 159), 151, 294 (n. 27), 304.
Centralization policy, **I**, 8 (n. 20); **II**, 62, 70, 92, 94, 325, 430.
Cessio, **II**, 343.
Chalk, **I**, 27, 66; **II**, 146 (n. 14).
Changeur-bancquier, **II**, 357, 358.
Chaplain, **I**, 39, 63.
Charcoal, **I**, 92 (n. 102), 94, 99, 102, 145 (n. 19), 254-256; **II**, 231, (n. 136), 397, 413; **III**, 103, 118.

Charge, see Weights, I, 72-79.

Cheese, I, 78, 114, 146, 533, 535-537; II, 101, 134, 161, 173, 210, 212, 251, 386, 390, 394, 395; III, 42, 49, 53, 55.

Cheese, *Cordewaens* cheese, I, 217 (n. 3).

Cheese, Dutch cheese, I, 78, 217, 224; II, 103, 122, 301.

Cheese, Flemish cheese, I, 31 (n. 75), 78, 158, 217-223; II, 8, 31 (n. 1), 102, 103, 170, 301; III, 20, 21, 43, 48, 52, 54, 99.

Cheese, *Isaex* cheese, I, 217 (n. 3).

Cheese, Italian cheese, I, 217 (n. 3).

Cheese, Tienen cheese, I, 217 (n. 3).

Churchwarden, I, 40, 49; II, 96 (n. 41).

Cinnamon, I, 28, 306, 314-317; II, 127.

Circulation of bills from hand to hand, II, 332, 334, 342-347, 350, 366, 367 (n. 177), 368.

Circulation of money (see also Velocity of circulation), II, 333, 415, 418, 420.

Citizenship, I, 62, 166; II, 66 (n. 28); III, 61.

Clause to order, II, 342.

Clause „payable to bearer", II, 334, 338-340, 342-348, 350, 358.

Clearing operation, II, 366, 368.

Clergy, I, 509; II, 86, 153, 175 (n.175), 307, 308, 383.

Cleynsteeker, see Stone cutter.

Climate, see Weather.

Cloth, I, 27, 46, 54, 55, 58, 103, 158, 269-272, 529-532; II, 10, 16, 132 (n. 109), 137, 164, 185, 186, 231, 274, 335, 339 (n. 35), 369, 373, 380, 381 (n. 53), 397, 419, 429 ; III, 42, 46, 49, 53, 54, 58, 91,

107.

Cloth, *Bellaert* cloth, II, 41, 110.

Cloth, Brabant cloth, I, 103; II, 11, 16, 25, 27, 41, 42, 46, 48, 52, 73, 124, 137, 314, 315 (n. 33), 429.

Cloth, Burgundian cloth, I, 103.

Cloth, carded cloth, II, 41.

Cloth, Dutch cloth, II, 16, 41, 45, 79 (n. 111), 164.

Cloth, English cloth, I, 53-55, 269; II, 12, 16, 26, 27, 38, 40, 41, 45-47, 51-53, 55, 56, 70, 73-75, 83, 105, 123, 124, 133, 136, 144-146, 164, 165, 181, 183-185, 218, 228-230, 238, 253, 258, 274, 315, 316, 330 (n. 113), 338, 373, 398, 399, 429, 430; III, 107.

Cloth, Flemish cloth, II, 12, 16, 27, 46, 48, 73, 124, 137, 178 (n. 191), 310, 314.

Cloth, gray cloth, I, 269; II, 137, 329 (n. 109).

Cloth, lining cloth, II, 137.

Cloth, cloth of Cologne, II, 52, 74.

Cloth, cloth of Hoorn, II, 99 (n. 63), 137, 258, 259, 274.

Cloth, cloth of Leiden, II, 68, 79 (n. 111), 80, 136, 145, 146, 164; III, 61.

Cloth, cloth of Malines, II, 16, 42, 69 (n. 46).

Cloth, cloth of Weert, II, 42, 134, 137, 162, 194, 229, 239, 258, 259, 274, 397, 422; III, 42, 43, 47, 48, 52, 55, 59, 90, 103, 118.

Cloth Dressers' craft, II, 197, 215.

Cloth dresser, cloth dressers' labourer, cloth shearer, I, 55; II, 18, 189 (n. 259), 197, 228-230, 300 (n. 53), 370 (n. 9).

Cloth finishing industry, I, 53, 269; II, 51 (n. 137), 70, 83, 100, 133, 138,

181 (n. 208), 184, 189, 197, 198, 229, 238, 258, 274, 379, 380.

Cloth guild, II, 33, 44; III, 62.

Cloth hall, I, 477; II, 10, 26 (n. 130), 33 (n. 9), 49, 50 (n. 124), 55 (n. 158), 63 (n. 10), 98, 132, (n. 108), 137, 165, 179 (n. 195), 185, 323,329; III, 70, 71.

Cloth industry, traditional export industry, I, 54, 529-531; II, 9, 10, 15, 16, 18, 19 (n. 93), 33, 38, 41, 45, 48, 49, 52, 55, 61, 63 (n. 10), 65 (n. 23), 67-74, 80, 81, 85, 86, 94, 95, 98, 100, 118, 136, 137, 140, 143, 145 (n. 9), 163, 164, 184-186, 195, 291 (n. 23), 294, 369-374, 376, 382, 395 (n. 18), 396, 397, 409, 410, 419, 429-431.

Clothing, I, 533, 538; II, 135, 187.

Clover, II, 299.

Cloves, I, 306, 325-328.

Coal, I, 79, 99, 100, 102 (n. 145); II, 189, 197.

Cobbler, I, 45, 48 (n. 130).

Coffer making (also trunk making), II, 70, 161, 188.

Coinage, see Money, I, 107-135; II, 78, 160.

Coin, see Money, I, 107-135.

Cole-seed, II, 299, 300 (n. 53).

Commons, II, 299.

Commission business, II, 276, 323, 326, 338, 378, 433.

Company, family company, II, 325, 326.

Company, joint-stock company, II, 325, 326.

Company, share company, II, 323, 325, 326, 378, 433.

Competition, competitive power, II, 72, 75, 78, 120, 122, 127, 128, 172,

184, 218, 258 (n. 99), 273, 301, 314, 318, 370.

Comuneros (revolt of the), II, 146, 177.

Conception, II, 405; III, 114, 115.

Concessio Carolina, II, 196.

Conference of Bruges, II, 230.

Conference of Cologne, II, 257 (n. 90).

Conservatism, II, 65, 67, 212.

Consulate of Bruges, II, 223.

Contract-wages, I. 333.

Convoy, II, 78, 105, 166, 255, 274, 277, 327.

Coolmand, see Measures of contents, I, 80-102.

Copper, I, 60, 67, 73, 77 (n. 63), 80, 84 (n. 87), 522, 523; II, 119 (n. 29), 122 (n. 48), 123 (n. 58), 126-131, 144, 145, 154, 158, 231, 317-321; III, 66.

Corn, I, 65, 66, 91 (n. 93), 189, 194.

Corn-measurer, I, 66, 91 (n. 93), 92; II, 121 (n. 39).

Corporation, see Craft guild.

Corporatism, corporate organization, I, 46; II, 14, 17, 64, 66, 71, 72, 132, 134, 135, 196, 198, 227, 230, 279, 313, 315, 323, 324, 326 (n. 91), 334, 371, 372, 374, 378, 379, 381-383, 385, 388, 395 (n. 18), 403, 404, 410, 419, 435.

Correlation coefficient, I, 9 (n. 23), 20, 167.

Correlation method, I, 166-168.

Corruption, II, 233.

Cost of living, II, 150, 385.

Cost of production, II, 72, 400.

Cost of transport, I, 22, 23, 145; II, 32 (n. 8), 102, 121, 310, 317, 321, 422.

Cost price, II, 370, 371, 434.

Council, court council, **II**, 84.

Council, great or large town council, **II**, 44, 72, 95.

Council, privy council, **II**, 148.

Council of Brabant, **II**, 58 (n. 173).

Council of Malines, **II**, 343 (n. 59).

Coutume, **II**, 343 (n. 59).

Cow, **I**, 28, 508; **II**, 31, 62, 175, 210, 211, 304.

Craft, craft guild, **I**, 39, 43, 46, 47, 49, 55, 64, 66 (n. 7), 103, 142, 150, 529, 532; **II**, 14 (n. 59), 43 (n. 81), 44-48, 68, 72, 85, 87, 93-95, 132, 133, 135, 152, 153, 193-198, 228, 280, 297 (n. 40), 310, 321 (n. 81), 356, 372, 374-376, 379 (n. 40, 41), 382, 395 (n. 18),

D

Daalder (see also *Joachim Thaler*), **II**, 225, 230, 231, 232 (n. 149), 241.

Dachwant, see Measures of length and area, **I**, 102-105.

Dairy products, **I**, 144; **II**, 62, 102, 103 (n. 86), 115, 122, 170, 211, 245, 298 (n. 45), 301, 390, 394-396, 398 (n. 26), 412, 417; **III**, 98.

Damask linen, **II**, 188.

Debasement, „Great Debasements", **II**, 163, 184, 204.

Debt, floating debt, **I**, 35, 61.

Debt, public debt, **II**, 214, 215, 242, 354, 355, 362.

Decimal system, **I**, 69-71.

Deflation, **I**, 112; **II**, 163, 333 (n. 2).

Democratic agitation, **II**, 371-373, 381, 429, 431.

Demographic revolution, **II**, 406.

Demography, see Population.

Denier, see Money, **I**, 107-135.

Deposit, **I**, 525, 528; **II**, 108, 222,

403, 404, 430, 435.

Crane, **I**, 60, 522, 524; **II**, 133, 255, 274.

Cromsteert, **II**, 36.

Crop-rotation, **II**, 299.

Cruzada, **II**, 206.

Crystal, crystal making, **II**, 188.

Currency, see Money, **I**, 107-135.

Currier, **II**, 242.

Curve of Gauss, **I**, 157.

Custom-house (of Danzig), **II**, 232.

Customs, **II**, 123 (n. 56), 184, 224.

Cyclical amplitude, **I**, 7, 9 (n. 23), 10, 12, 15-17, 19, 20, 161, 165; **II**, 209, 390-405.

Cyclical fluctuation, **I**, 163 (n. 70), 164; **II**, 390-405, 408.

265 (n. 161), 353 (n. 103), 359, 367 (n. 178).

Deposit from fair to fair, **II**, 166, 202, 332, 353.

Devaluation, **I**, 13, 109, 111, 121, 122, 156, 511 (n. 1); **II**, 10, 12, 13, 16, 29, 38, 39 (n. 44), 41, 43 (n. 80), 47, 67, 74 (n. 75), 80-83, 95-97, 105, 106, 148, 163, 176, 178, 182-185, 211, 231, 241, 251, 263-266, 311, 333 (n. 2), 356, 366 (n. 171), 372, 381, 416, 417, 420.

Diamond cutter, **II**, 378.

Digger, **II**, 175 (n. 177), 197, 304.

Dike, **II**, 33, 249, 269, 271, 303.

Discount, **II**, 300 (n. 55), 332, 345, 349-352, 355 (n. 115), 360, 364, 368, 434.

Dispersion, **I**, 146, 148, 150, 156, 157.

Distribution, **II**, 99, 129, 324, 335.

Diversification of production, **II**, 374-376, 424, 430, 434.

Division of labour, **II**, 296, 371, 422.

Docker, **II**, 100 (n. 72).

Drachm, see Weights, **I**, 72-79.

Draff, **I**, 91.

Draft-animal, **II**, 34 (n. 19), 296, 297.

Douzaine, **II**, 147.

Draper, **II**, 15, 16, 68, 146, 175, 176, 198, 323, 329, 334 (n. 10), 338, 373 (n. 17), 380.

Drapery, new light drapery, **II**, 11, 15, 31, 41, 42, 62, 68, 137, 180, 186, 187, 190, 198, 370, 377, 378, 380.

Drapery, serge drapery, **I**, 54; **II**, 68.

Dresser, see Cloth dresser.

Drought, **I**, 550-562.

Drugget, **II**, 187.

Dry herring, see Smoked herring.

Ducat, **II**, 266.

Dumping, **II**, 163 (n. 125).

Dung, pidgeon dung, **II**, 299 (n. 46).

Duty, **II**, 31, 67, 249, 373.

Dyer and Dyers' labourer, **II**, 18, 118, 185, 193, 228, 229, 261 (n.130), 370 (n. 9).

Dyes, **II**, 21.

E

Easterling, **I**, 73; **II**, 23, 301, 313.

Eastland company, **II**, 224.

Ecu, see Money, **I**, 107-135; **II**, 53, 147, 182, 200 (n. 322).

Ecu de marc, see Money, **I**, 107-135; **II**, 367.

Education, **II**, 331, 378.

Effraction, **I**, 15 (n. 42).

Egg, **I**, 27, 144, 146, 147, 204-209, 533, 535-537; **II**, 9, 210, 394, 395; **III**, 99.

Elasticity of demand, **II**, 390, 393, 398.

Elasticity of supply, **II**, 383.

Elimination of systematic errors, **I**, 142, 143, 148, 149, 333.

Ell, see Measures of length and area, **I**, 102-105.

Embargo, **II**, 101, 121, 144, 145, 159, 182 (n. 216), 214, 228, 237, 238, 242, 250, 260, 277, 282, 322, 392, 397, 402, 411, 419.

Embroiderer, **I**, 50 (n. 135); **II**, 81, 195 (n. 293), 226, 261 (n. 129).

Embroidery, **II**, 70, 135 (n. 128), 138, 181, 187, 380.

Emigration, **I**, 9, 49, 65 (n. 23), 66, 67, 69, 90 (n. 9), 100 (n. 69), 114, 134, 139, 161, 162 (n. 116), 219, 231, 236, 238, 242, 255, 261-263, 272, 273, 278, 279, 290, 294, 373, 387, 417, 420, 432.

Emmer, see Measures of contents, **I**, 80-102.

Employment, **I**, 539-544; **II**, 36, 44, 65, 81, 96, 117, 118, 133 (n. 118), 134, 138, 146 (n. 14), 150, 162, 175, 176, 192-194, 197, 198, 212, 219, 227, 230, 290 (n. 9), 375, 379 (n. 40), 381 (n. 53), 383, 385, 386, 387 (n. 73), 400, 401, 403, 414; **III**, 90, 93.

Endorsement, **II**, 332, 340, 348, 349, 364, 368, 434.

Epidemics, **II**, 15, 48 (n. 112), 61, 69, 162, 246, 247 (n. 9), 248, 250, 289, 293, 370, 404-406, 419.

150

Episcopal commissioner, I, 24, 25.

Escomesse, II, 365.

Estamette, II, 187.

Evene, see Oats and Rough oats.

Exchange, bill of exchange, II, 29, 57, 163, 203, 205 (n. 361), 221 (n. 73), 243, 265-267, 281, 282, 322, 332, 339, 340, 341 (n. 50), 344-352, 358-360, 368, 433.

Exchange, Goods Exchange, Financial *Bourse*), I, 155; II, 202, 222, 234, 238, 263, 265 (n. 161), 267, 330, 331, 345, 346, 353, 355, 359, 364-366, 433, 434.

Exchange arbitrage, II, 57, 202, 265, 339, 352, 353, 359, 361, 363, 364.

Exchange market, I, 119, 120; II, 29, 57, 58, 111, 204, 242, 243, 264-266, 282, 330, 346, 361, 367.

Exchange money, see Money, I, 107-135.

Exchange rate, I, 62, 119-121, 160; II, 14, 16, 29, 184, 201, 203, 204, 239, 241, 243, 256, 264-266, 281, 340, 341 (n. 50), 360, 365, 366, 367 (n. 174); III, 77, 78.

Exchange stall, II, 108, 356.

Exchequer, I, 8, 12, 68.

Excise duty, I, 22, 55, 60, 61, 65, 81, 145 (n. 18), 294, 510, 520, 521; II, 10 (n. 18), 48, 80 (n. 118), 89 (n. 2), 94, 96 (n. 38), 99, 106, 138 (n. 146), 145, 152, 212 (n. 12), 215, 229, 257, 258, 261 (n. 129), 369 (n. 3), 396 (n. 22); III, 61, 64, 65.

Exploitation of agriculture, exploitation unit, I, 509; II, 35, 36 61, 65 (n. 23), 67, 117, 175, 209, 290-292, 294, 296 (n. 32, 33), 302-308, 378, 421.

F

Factory, Hanseatic factory, II, 12, 50, 51, 219, 224, 274.

Factory of Portuguese spices, II, 154, 155, 217 (n. 51).

Faggot (*mutsaert*), I, 42, 433-438, 447, 448, 470-475.

Fair, passim.

Fallow land, II, 298, 299.

Family coefficient, I, 62.

Farmer, large farmer, I, 50; II, 35, 65 (n. 21), 91, 92, 115 (n. 10), 167, 174-176, 304-308, 400-402, 435.

Farmer, small farmer, I, 50; II, 64, 65, 66, 295, 296, 302-308, 400.

Farmer, unfree farmer, I, 38, 40 (n. 109), 53, 489-492; II, 117, 174, 290; III, 109.

Fashion, I, 185, 187, 386.

Feitoria de Flandres, II, 129.

Fellow ship of Antwerp skippers trading with England, II, 226, 257.

Fellow ship of Merchant Adventurers, see Merchant Adventurers.

Feudalism, II, 291.

Fines, II, 61 (n. 2).

Firewood, I, 29, 30, 42, 68, 70, 94, 95, 101, 102, 238-241, 333; II, 116, 118, 173, 231 (n. 136), 246, 259, 260, 299, 304 (n. 73), 385, 397, 398, 412, 414-416; III, 56, 57.

Fiscal policy, II, 66, 67, 86, 89, 93, 236, 239.

Fish, I, 277 (n. 2), 534-537; II, 20, 251, 293.

Fisher, II, 165, 175 (n. 177), 304.

Fishing, I, 278; II, 138, 145, 164, 165, 240.

Flax, I, 77, 79, 477; II, 8, 9, 15 (n. 68), 31, 62, 63, 64 (n. 19), 116, 170, 197, 210, 299, 301, 303, 304, 317 (n. 46), 394, 397, 409, 410, 412, 414-417, 434; III, 42, 43, 100.

Flax, Flemish flax, I, 77, 79, 233-237; II, 120, 377.

Flax, Kempen flax, I, 79; II, 116.

Flax, Zeeland flax, I, 77, 79, 233; II, 120.

Flax growing, I, 233; II, 298, 303, 304.

Fleet, Antwerp commercial fleet, II, 226.

Flood, I, 287, 550-562; II, 33, 43 (n. 78), 62, 78, 165, 167, 174 (n. 171), 211, 249, 272 (n. 18), 292.

Fodder, see Cattle fodder.

Fondaco dei Tedeschi, II, 76 (n. 91), 82.

G

Gale, I, 550-562.

Galley, II, 20, 50, 103, 124, 127, 154, 311 (n. 14).

Gang, see Measures of contents, I, 80-102.

Garbeleur, I, 307.

Garden worker, II, 197.

Gate-keeper, I, 39.

Gelte, see Measures of contents, I, 80-102.

Gemete, see Measures of length and area, I, 102-105.

Ginger, I, 306, 311-314; II, 154, 155 (n. 75).

Foot, see Measures of length and area, I, 102-105.

Forest, see Wood.

Forester, II, 94, 95.

Franc, II, 53.

Fraud, I, 52, 55, 58-60, 77, 94, 103, 111; II, 38 (n. 39), 93, 123 (n. 56), 152, 230, 232 (n. 149), 266, 356, 365 (n. 163), 416, 417.

Freight, I, 23, 57; II, 102, 154, 223, 317 (n. 46), 322.

Frequency, I, 145, 147-151, 157, 160, 168, 333, 336, 525; II, 32,33.

Frost, I, 550-562.

Fruit, I, 533, 535-537; II, 385.

Fuller, II, 10, 15-17, 18 (n. 88), 49 (n. 120), 68, 69, 98, 118, 152, 370 (n. 9), 382.

Fur, II, 70, 71, 72 (n. 67), 120.

Furier, fur worker, II, 71, 81, 135 (n. 126), 195 (n. 293), 341 (n. 47).

Fury, II, 245, 259, 264, 270.

Fustian, II, 110, 186, 188.

Futures, business in futures, II, 330 (n. 113), 366.

Glass, see Measures of contents, I, 80-102.

Glass maker, glass making, II, 188, 378.

Glazier, glazing, II, 188, 226.

Glove, glove maker, II, 70, 81, 161.

Gold, I, 75 (n. 55), 78, 107-135; II, 16, 26, 29, 30, 57 (n. 169), 74 (n. 75), 78, 80, 82 (n. 129), 114, 124-126, 148, 159, 177, 200, 203, 281, 317, 338 (n. 26), 367 (n. 178), 409, 412, 415; III, 118.

Gold equivalent, see Money, I, 107-135; III, 94, 119.

Gold currency rate, **II**, 29, 41, 109, 126, 147, 148, 163, 200, 201, 203, 260, 338, 356, 409, 415.

Gold-silver ratio, **II**, 24 (n. 120), 29, 124, 125, 148, 160, 178, 309, 311, 363.

Goldsmith, **I**, 68, 73; **II**, 161, 226, 368.

Gold thread, **I**, 181, 224.

Gothic architecture, **II**, 44 (n. 83), 72, 387 (n. 72).

Grain, passim.

Grain, see Weights, **I**, 72-79.

Grain Buyers'guild, **II**, 172 (n. 165).

Grain scales of Amsterdam, **I**, 93.

Grain trade, **II**, 24 (n. 116), 32, 35 (n. 23), 61, 90, 96, 97, 101, 102, 114, 119-123, 144, 150, 152, 157 (n. 95), 167, 171, 172, 182 (n. 214), 209, 211, 217-219, 225, 231, 232, 245, 246, 250, 251, 257, 263, 282, 302, 312, 313, 317 (n. 46), 318 (n. 49), 320 (n. 55), 366, 390, 392 (n. 9), 398, 399 (n. 28), 402, 409, 412, 413, 417, 434.

Grease, **I**, 31.

Groat (*groot*), see Money, **I**, 107-135.

Grocer, **I**, 31.

Groesgeld, **II**, 168-170.

Gruit, **I**, 228.

Guarantee of bills (*aval*), **II**, 348, 349 (n. 78), 368.

Guardian, **I**, 294.

Guild, see Craft guild.

Guild of St. Luke, **II**, 133, 226.

Guilder, see Money, **I**, 107-135.

Gutting technique, **I**, 277, 278.

H

Haagmuntindustrie, see Minting industry.

Haberdasher (also finisher, shearer), **II**, 76 (n. 92), 138 (n. 150).

Hacienda real de Castilla, **II**, 204 (n. 346), 213 (n. 18).

Hail, **I**, 550-562.

Halster, see Measures of contents, **I**, 80-102.

Hamburg banco, see Money, **I**, 107-135.

Handworker, **I**, 42, 49, 50, 333; **II**, 32, 64, 65, 90, 91, 117, 118, 136 (n. 131), 150, 153, 175, 176, 196, 197, 210, 212, 213, 258, 303-306, 378, 400; **III**, 44-47, 54-59, 90, 91, 112, 113.

Hansa House, **II**, 225, 227, 254.

Hanseatic Factory, see Factory.

Hanse Tag, **II**, 50, 120 (n. 32).

Harincbuys, see Herring fleet.

Harpsichord maker, **II**, 226.

Harvest year, **I**, 143-145, 171, 183 (n. 1); **II**, 401, 402.

Hat making, **II**, 70.

Hay, **II**, 32.

Haver, see Oats.

Heaped measure, **I**, 71, 90, 98.

Hearth, **I**, 62, 151, 161; **II**, 35 (n. 22), 37, 66 (n. 26), 113, 139 (n. 159), 250.

Heat, **I**, 550-560.

Heating, **I**, 533, 538.

Hectare, see Measures of length and area, **I**, 102-105.

Hellingvat, see Measures of contents, I, 80-102.

Hellingweert, see Measures of contents, I, 80-102.

Herring, I, 26, 100, 114, 158, 277-287; II, 25, 43, 78, 145, 165, 240, 317 (n. 46), 398, 422; III, 22, 23, 42, 43, 48, 49, 56, 57, 104, 118.

Herring, Brabant herring (*Antwerpsche, Mechelsche, Bossche brand*), I, 101; II, 42, 78, 79 (n. 108), 422.

Herring, Dutch herring, I, 101; II, 75.

Herring, finishing industry, I, 277, 278, 287; II, 42, 43 (n. 78), 50, 70, 75, 78, 100, 138, 145, 164, 165, 251, 422, 423.

Herring, Flemish herring, I, 101; II, 422.

Herring, Scania herring, I, 101, 277, 278; II, 75, 78, 422.

Herring fleet, I, 278; II, 165 (n. 140).

Herring packer, II, 97.

Hesse House, II, 192 (n. 276), 328.

Hide, II, 72 (n. 67), 251.

Hoarding, II, 30, 148.

Honey, II, 120.

Hooreken (*heureken*), see Cloth of Hoorn.

Hop, hop growing, I, 79, 98, 228-232, 294; II, 31, 62, 116, 170, 210, 301, 317 (n. 46), 318, 412.

Hop beer, I, 228, 229; II, 23, 31, 301.

Horse, horse breeding, I, 508; II, 31, 34, 62, 115 (n. 11), 211, 297.

Hundred penny tax, see Tax.

Hundred Years war, II, 63, 75, 312-314.

Hydographic change, II, 55, 430.

Hygiene, II, 291 (n. 12), 405.

I

Iconoclastic revolt, II, 211, 212, 234, 235, 237, 240, 241.

Immigration, II, 13, 16 (n. 77), 38 (n. 40), 41 (n. 60), 45, 64, 66, 68, 135, 139, 191 (n. 270), 258, 363, 379 (n. 40), 404; III, 61.

Imposition, II, 86, 94.

Inch, see Measures of length and area, I, 102-105.

Income, I, 51, 488-507, 511-520, 522, 524, 539-544; II, 36, 66, 75, 91, 92, 99, 117, 118, 134, 136, 138, 141, 150, 151, 173-176, 214, 219, 227, 249, 261, 272, 290, 292-294, 296, 304-308, 329, 374, 378, 379, 382-388, 390, 395 (n. 22), 400-405, 410, 418, 434; III, 61, 65, 69, 72-74, 89, 90, 93.

Income elasticity of demand, II, 8, 9, 289, 394-396, 410, 414, 417, 424.

Indexical averages (*moyennes indicielles*), I, 159, 477-487.

Index numbers (method of the), I, 152-161.

Industrial crop, II, 62, 116, 118, 210, 293, 298, 301, 302, 318 (n. 49), 394, 410, 413, 431, 433; III, 101.

Industrialization, II, 8, 176, 191, 232, 306.

Industrial revolution, I, 117 (n. 32); II, 316, 425, 436.

Industry, cloth industry, see Cloth.

Industry, export industry, II, 17, 70, 72 (n. 67), 73, 143, 163, 189, 238, 280, 370, 378, 382-385, 394, 396,

397, 409, 410, 416, 419, 422; **III**, 61.

Industry, local industry, **II**, 17, 70.

Industry, rural industry, **II**, 8, 33, 41, 63 (n. 10), 89, 91, 117, 118, 137, 138, 175, 176, 186, 190, 209, 212, 249, 293, 372, 373 (n. 17), 413, 415, 421, 431, 434.

Industry, specialized industry, **II**, 70-73, 80, 81, 99, 100, 187, 191, 195, 196, 252, 273, 371, 376-378, 380, 430, 432, 434.

Inertia of wages, **II**, 15, 64, 382.

Inflation, **I**, 156, 210; **II**, 81, 225, 413, 420-422, 435.

Infra-structure, **II**, 218.

Ingels, see Weights, **I**, 72-79.

Inn, innkeeper, **I**, 31, 67, 82, 175 (n. 177); **II**, 324, 334 (n. 10).

Innovation, technical innovation, **II**, 191, 209, 287, 291, 295-302, 316, 318, 320, 325 (n. 88), 327-332, 348, 352, 354-360, 369, 371, 375-377, 386 (n. 71), 419, 422-425, 433.

Inquisition, **II**, 220, 233.

Insolvency, **II**, 247.

Insurance, **II**, 202, 222, 239, 327, 365.

Insurance (codification of maritime insurance law), **II**, 366.

Institutional price, **I**, 29.

Intensive husbandry, **II**, 295, 296 (n. 33), 298-300, 302, 377, 431.

Intercursus malus, **II**, 123, 230.

Interest, interest rate, **I**, 34, 35, 58, 61, 141, 150, 525-528; **II**, 56, 57, 84, 85, 106, 109, 140, 141, 147, 149, 150, 199, 200, 203-205, 213 (n. 18), 214, 242, 332, 335, 337, 340, 349 (n. 83, 85), 350, 351 (n. 92), 352-355, 358, 360-364, 399, 434; **III**, 81, 82. 107.

International price arbitrage, **I**, 120, 121.

Interpolation, **I**, 150, 151, 189.

Investment, **I**, 32, 33, 37, 43, 477; **II**, 56, 66, 85, 108, 116, 134, 141, 149, 160, 161, 174, 179, 192, 193, 199, 200, 222, 224, 253, 270, 281, 296, 307, 308, 311, 316, 322, 355, 359, 361-363, 374, 375, 380, 386, 396 (n. 22), 399, 412, 414, 415, 421, 423, 431.

Iron, **I**, 94; **II**, 180, 189, 319.

J

Jew, **II**, 203.

Jewel, **II**, 57 (n. 170), 87.

Jeweller, **I**, 68, 73.

Joachim Thaler (see also *Daalder*), **II**, 160.

Joiner, **II**, 193.

Journeyman, **I**, 46, 47 (n. 129), 48, 50, 334, 336-365, 393-420, 458-463; **II**, 68, 135, 195, 196, 197 (n. 302), 230, 275, 279, 379, 403, 434.

Joyeuse Entrée, **II**, 94, 193.

Judicial officer, **I**, 10, 11.

Juperken, see Measures of contents, **I**, 80-102.

Juros, **II**, 215.

K

Kaufmannsmark (of Cologne), see Weights, I, 72-79.
Kerke, see Weights, I, 72-79.
Kerseys, II, 181, 186, 187.

Kindeke, see Measures of contents, I, 80-102.
Knife, II, 138 (n. 154).
Knol beer, *Koyte* beer, see Beer.

L

Labourer, see Handworker.
Lamb, I, 29, 51 (n. 141); II, 62 (n. 6).
Landowner, large landowner, II, 35, 62, 65, 91, 92 (n. 19), 116-118, 167, 174, 270, 306-308, 401, 402, 435.
Larghezza, II, 29, 201, 239, 243, 265-267, 281, 343 (n. 60).
Last of Amsterdam, see Measures of contents, I, 80-102.
Law of diminishing returns, II, 35, 61, 289-293, 295, 312, 316, 369, 424.
Law of Gresham (so-called), I, 112.
Law of King, II, 35 (n. 23), 402, 417.
Law of probability (law of the great numbers), I, 29, 53, 142, 149-151, 154, 155; II, 365.
Layer of cobbles, I, 333.
Lead, I, 79.
League, Holy league II, 119.
League of Cambrai, II, 127, 129.
League of Schmalkalden, II, 159, 164, 201, 204.
Lease, I, 18 (n. 45), 32-34, 37, 40 (n. 109), 52 (n. 143); II, 7, 77 (n. 93), 100 (n. 71), 103 (n. 91), 270 (n. 6).
Least squares (method of), I, 162.
Leather, II, 70, 71, 80 (n. 118), 138, 188, 251.
Leather worker, II, 81.
Letter cutter, II, 226.
Letter obligatory (see also Bond),

II, 332-334, 338-340, 342-352, 358, 359, 368.
Licence, II, 182 (n. 216), 253, 255, 274, 365.
Light, I, 533, 538.
Light drapery, see Drapery.
Lime, lime preparation, I, 99, 101, 144, 262-268; II, 189, 227, 229, 319 (n. 54), 397; III, 46-49, 54, 55, 58, 59, 103, 118.
Lime-kiln, I, 257, 262.
Linen, I, 27, 41, 55, 103, 233, 273-276, 450-456, 470-475; II, 8, 9, 138 (n. 146), 145, 178 (n. 191), 181, 188, 190 212 (n. 12), 215, 229, 256-258, 299, 394, 405, 410; III, 61.
Linen, Dutch linen, II, 190.
Linen, Flemish linen, II, 89 (n. 2), 181, 190, 252, 253, 278, 318, 377, 394 (n. 17); III, 61.
Linen, Kempen coarse linen, I, 273; II, 89, 298 (n. 45).
Linen, Westphalian linen, II, 15 (n. 68).
Linen weaver, I, 450-458; II, 42, 81, 89, 162, 175 (n. 177), 229, 304, 377, 403, 405, 420, 422; III, 38-43, 46-49, 56, 57, 63, 90, 91, 110.
Linen weaving industry, I, 55, 273; II, 8, 12, 15, 33, 42, 62, 63, 70, 80 (n. 118), 81 (n. 124), 116, 117, 138, 175, 210, 212, 215, 225, 236,

239, 247, 249, 252, 253, 262, 278, 279, 298 (n. 45), 303, 375-377, 378 (n. 36), 394, 415, 420.

Linie, see Measures of length and area, **I**, 102-105.

Lining, **I**, 530-531.

„Link" money, see Money, **I**, 107-135; **II**, 36.

Linseed, linseed oil, **I**, 81; **II**, 116.

„Little Ice Period", **II**, 209, 414 (n. 9).

Livestock, **I**, 507, 508; **II**, 211, 248, 396, 417.

Loan, **I**, 34-36, 58, 61, 141, 150, 525, 526; **II**, 25 (n. 123), 28-30, 56-58, 84-87, 106-109, 111, 140-142, 147-149, 199, 200, 204-206, 214, 242, 264 (n. 155), 267, 332, 337, 349 (n. 83), 352-355, 361, 362, 399, 414, 415; **III**, 81, 82, 107.

Logarithmic conversion, **I**, 152-162, 167, 168.

Logarithmic scale, **I**, 156, 167, 168.

Logistic growth graph, **II**, 271.

Loists, **II**, 153.

Lombard, **II**, 58, 85, 87, 231 (n. 136), 335.

Long-distance trade, see Trade.

Loom, **II**, 63 (n. 10), 175, 373 (n. 17), 380.

Loop, see Measures of contents, **I**, 80-102.

Loot, see Weights, **I**, 72-79.

Lottery, **II**, 192, 202, 364, 365.

Lutheranism, **II**, 153, 162 (n. 124), 384.

Luxury article, **II**, 21, 55, 70, 76, 158, 187, 310, 312, 318, 375, 386, 395, 396, 398, 403, 415 (n. 13).

Luxury industry, **I**, 295; **II**, 70, 181, 187, 188, 224, 226, 273, 374, 377.

Luxury textiles, **I**, 104 (n. 152); **II**, 21, 135, 386.

M

Maendagsche Raed, see Council, large town council.

Maestrazgos, **II**, 206 (n. 366).

Magnus Intercursus, **II**, 123, 133.

Maid, **I**, 40, 41, 50, 217 (n. 1); **II**, 303, 304.

Majolica tile, **II**, 226, 378.

Malaguette - pepper, **II**, 78, 105, 423.

Malestroit effect, **I**, 166, 121, 122.

Malt, **I**, 91.

Manufacture, **II**, 197, 381.

Manure, **II**, 168, 298, 299.

Marginal enterprise, **II**, 63, 65, 66, 117, 164, 301.

Marketing policy, marketing orgazation, **I**, 30, 31; **II**, 27, 132,

323, 324, 328-330, 333-336.

Mark weight (of Cologne, of Flanders, of Paris, and Troy weight), see Weights, **I**, 72-79.

Marriage, **II**, 405, 406 (n. 41); **III**, 114, 115.

Mason, **I**, 40 (n. 108), 43, 45, 46, 47 (n. 129), 48 (n. 129), 333 (n. 2), 336-349, 393-405, 439-440, 457-469, 539-544; **II**, 43, 135 (n. 126), 162, 193-196, 259, 275, 403, 404; **III**, 32, 33, 38-50, 53-59, 90-92, 94, 95, 111.

Masons' labourer, **I**, 378-392, 421-432, 445, 446, 457-469, 539-544; **II**, 197, 229, 275, 386, 404; **III**,

38, 39, 44-47, 52-55, 90-92, 112.

Master, mastership, **I**, 46, 47 (n. 129), 50, 80, 334, 336-365, 393-420, 458-463; **II**, 98, 118, 135, 195-198, 258, 259, 275, 279, 323, 328, 379, 403, 434.

Meat, **I**, 29, 158, 225-227, 287, 535-537; **II**, 9, 86, 115, 161, 173, 194, 210-212, 249, 298 (n. 45), 385, 386, 394-396, 412; **III**, 46, 47, 54, 55, 87, 98, 99.

Median average, **I**, 150, 161, 163, 166, 457-475.

Medicine, **II**, 291 (n. 12), 405.

Mercenary, see Army.

Mercer, **I**, 49 (n. 131), 307; **II**, 132, 133.

Merchant, big merchant family, **II**, 130, 148, 149, 160, 181, 216, 231, 257, 319-321, 325, 328, 425, 432.

Merchant, small merchant, **II**, 132, 191, 226, 310, 315, 321-324, 326, 328, 331, 334, 338, 339, 365, 366 (n. 171), 378, 433.

Merchant Adventurers (Fellowship of the), **II**, 22, 23, 27, 51 (n. 137), 53, 74, 103, 105, 123, 165, 186, 203 (n. 342), 228-230, 237, 238, 259, 323 (n. 75), 345 (n. 67), 431.

Merchant-banker, **II**, 57, 84 (n. 141), 111, 131, 148, 149, 201, 202, 206 (n. 366), 221 (n. 71), 241, 264, 276 (n. 37), 280, 281, 311, 320, 321, 325, 339, 352, 353, 359, 361, 375.

Merchant-entrepreneur, **II**, 371, 425.

Mercuriale, **I**, 5, 174; **II**, 382, 405; **III**, 14, 16, 17.

Messe, **II**, 24, 25, 26, 315, 321.

Messenger, **II**, 197.

Mesure comble, *mesure rase*, see Measures of contents, **I**, 80-102.

Metal industry, **II**, 70, 71.

Metallic parity, **I**, 120.

Métayage, **I**, 18, 41, 52; **II**, 37.

Metereology, see Weather.

Meze, see Measures of contents, **I**, 80-102.

Middle class, **II**, 72, 85, 86, 95, 96, 132, 149-153, 194, 196 (n. 299), 220, 227, 231, 233, 308, 374, 375, 378, 379, 382-386, 395 (n. 18), 405, 420, 430-432, 434.

Middleman, see Broker.

Midwife, **I**, 63.

Migration, **II**, 66 (n. 28), 290, 291, 293.

Mile, see Measures of length and area, **I**, 102-105.

Militias, urban militias, **II**, 34 (n. 19), 297.

Milk, **I**, 533, 535-537.

Miller, **I**, 52; **II**, 175 (n. 177), 304.

Millstone, **II**, 317 (n. 46).

Mine, mining, **II**, 82, 124, 126, 192, 311, 320, 321 (n. 60).

Mint, **II**, 20 (n. 102), 26, 38 (n. 39), 54 (n. 153), 125, 148, 160.

Minting industry, **I**, 111 (n. 17); **II**, 160, 230, 409, 416, 417.

Mint-parity, **I**, 119, 161.

Mirror making, **II**, 188, 226, 378.

Mite, see Money, **I**, 107-135.

Mode (average), **I**, 148, 149, 457-475; **II**, 32, 33.

Money-changer, **II**, 85, 107-109, 341, 342, 355-357, 358 (n. 131).

Money market, **I**, 35, 36, 525-527; **II**, 28, 29, 56-58, 84-87, 106, 109-111, 140-143, 146-150, 177, 178, 192, 199-207, 220-222, 239-243, 263-267, 276, 277, 280-282, 332, 358, 360-368, 399, 412, 414-416, 431, 432, 434; **III**, 82, 106.

Money trade, **II**, 351, 358, 359.

Monopoly, **I**, 278, 288 (n. 6), 295;
II, 22, 25, 58, 72, 74, 105, 127-131,
143, 153-157, 161, 210 (n. 4), 238,
257, 261 (n. 127), 281, 299 (n. 46),
319, 320, 424, 431.
Mont de Piété, **II**, 336.
Moratorium, **II**, 203, 205, 263.
Mortality, mortality rate, **I**, 166;
II, 43 (n. 80), 90, 227, 261, 262,
291, 292, 387, 400, 404, 405, 417.
Mortar, see Lime.
Mottoen, mouton, see Money, **I**,
107-135.
Moving average (method of), **I**,
162-164, 166; **III**, 28, 29.
Moving median (method of), **I**, 166.
Mower, **I**, 333.
Moyenne indicielle, see Indexical
average.
Mudde, muddeke, see Measures of
contents, **I**, 80-102.
Myrtle-berry, **I**, 228.
Myte, see Measures of contents, **I**,
80-102.

N

Nagel, see Weights, **I**, 72-79.
Nail, nail making, **II**, 138, 195
(n. 293).
Narva company, **II**, 253, 340.
Nation (*natie*), **II**, 103, 104, 119,
132, 198, 237 (n. 174), 254, 257,
354, 366, 367 (n. 178).
Navigation, **II**, 78, 114, 120, 130,
154-158, 165, 171, 179, 182, 216,
224, 229, 237, 239, 250, 255, 257,
265, 273, 278, 311, 326-328, 332,
413.
Negotiability, **II**, 340-349, 433.
Neutrality, **II**, 114, 119, 141, 257.
New drapery, see Drapery.
New Town project, **II**, 189, 193.
Nobel, **II**, 53.
Nobility, **I**, 509; **II**, 58, 62, 92, 175
(n. 175), 233, 306 (n. 83), 307, 308,
383, 421 (n. 19).
Nutrition, **II**, 289, 293, 294, 404,
405.

O

Oak, **I**, 254; **II**, 319 (n. 54).
Oats (*avena sativa, witte evene*), **I**,
7, 9, 21, 70, 71, 85-94, 98, 194-198;
II, 20, 32, 297, 298 (n. 41), 392;
III, 18, 19, 96.
Oil, **I**, 29, 81, 83, 84 (n. 86), 535-
537; **II**, 116.
Oil cake, **II**, 116.
Onion, **II**, 317 (n. 46).
Open-field system, **II**, 299 (n. 48).
Organ builder, **II**, 226.
Ounce, see Weights, **I**, 72-79.
Ou scild, see Money, **I**, 107-135.
Overvaluation, **II**, 74 (n. 75), 78,
80-82, 104, 105, 160, 182, 409,
411, 430.
Oxen, fat oxen, **I**, 28, 508; **II**, 31,
34 (n. 19), 54 (n. 154), 62, 115,
175, 210, 211, 245, 255, 297, 301,
304.
Oxhoofd, see Measures of contents,
I, 80-102.

P

Pacification of Ghent, II, 245, 255.

Pack thread, II, 138 (n. 154).

Painter, painting, I, 504 (n. 8); II, 70, 81, 133, 176, 188, 189, 193, 226, 305.

Pamphlet, II, 153.

Parity, see Metallic parity and Mint-parity.

Particularism, I, 65; II, 94, 373.

Pasture, II, 115.

Patrician, II, 72, 188, 375.

Pauperism, II, 162, 176, 290.

Paving stone, I, 257.

Pawn-broker, pawn-broking, II, 85, 86, 231, 335, 336.

Peace of Arras, II, 101.

Peace of Bruges, II, 96, 101.

Peace of Cambrai (Paix des Dames), II, 150, 173, 180.

Peace of Cateau-Cambrésis, II, 215, 216, 221-228.

Peace of Copenhagen, II, 79, 102.

Peace of Frankfurt, II, 97.

Peace of Montils-les-Tours, II, 97.

Peace of Nijmegen, II, 253.

Peace of Passau, II, 213.

Peace of Speyer, II, 158, 171, 218, 431.

Peas, I, 26, 29, 31 (n. 76), 98, 158, 199-203; III, 24, 25, 96.

Peasants' revolt, 145, 159, 164.

Peat, I, 28, 30, 66, 92 (n. 102), 95, 100, 101, 145 (n. 19); II, 189, 197, 231 (n. 136), 246, 251, 319 (n. 54).

Peat cutter, I, 30.

Peat carrier, I, 66; II, 132.

Peeter, see Money, I, 107-135.

Penny (of England), II, 38 (n. 39).

Pepper, I, 28, 306-310; II, 57 (n.169), 78, 127-129, 140, 154-156, 257, 395, 423, 424; III, 20, 21, 42, 43, 46, 47, 104, 118.

Pest, see Epidemics.

Picker, II, 370 (n. 9).

Pignoel, see Measures of contents, I, 80-102.

Pig, I, 28.

Pin making, II, 138, 152.

Pint, see Measures of contents, I, 80-102.

Pipe, see Measures of contents, I, 80-102.

Piracy, II, 37, 38, 40, 56, 74, 97, 144, 158, 165, 214, 229, 237, 239, 277, 282, 322, 327.

Plack, see Money, I, 107-135.

Plough, II, 297.

Polder, I, 33, 477-482, 550, 552, 557; II, 7, 65, 93, 117, 167, 174 (n. 171), 175, 211, 269, 271, 272, 299 (n. 48); III, 71.

Polyculture, II, 302.

Population, I, 546-548; II, 7, 8, 21, 31-37, 61, 65-69, 75, 79 (n. 114), 81, 90-92, 99-101, 113, 114, 116-119, 122, 132, 133, 139, 150, 162, 165, 167, 171-173, 175, 179, 194, 209, 220, 226 (n. 100), 227, 247 (n. 9), 249, 250, 253, 261, 262, 269, 271-273, 276, 279 (n. 55), 289-296, 302, 303, 305 (n. 78), 312, 370, 378, 379 (n. 41), 382, 383, 390, 396, 397, 400, 405-414, 416, 418, 419, 420, 430, 433-435.

Population (theory of), II, 289-292, 295, 407.

Porter, II, 132, 197, 198, 380 (n. 43).

Port organization, I, 522; II, 132, 133, 135, 192, 196, 198, 274, 326, 327.

Post, **II**, 328.

Potter, **II**, 324 (n. 81).

Poultry, **I**, 29.

Pound, pound Artois, pound Brabant groats, pound Brabant payment, pound Flemish groats, pound Flemish payment, pound old groats, pound Parisis, see Money, **I**, 107-135.

Pound, pound of Brabant, pound of Flanders, see Weights, **I**, 72-79.

Poverty, policy on poverty, **II**, 162, 163, 214.

Poverty, poverty percentage, poverty index, **II**, 35 (n. 22), 36 (n. 25), 37, 70, 72, 90, 113, 139, 151, 162 (n. 122), 194, 237, 294, 306.

Prägungsmark of Cologne, see Weights, **I**, 72-79.

Precious metal, **I**, 73, 116, 117, 121-123; **II**, 24, 54 (n. 153), 59, 111, 114, 125, 178, 180 (n. 202), 201, 202, 204, 206, 241, 265, 363, 377, 407, 409, 412 (n. 8), 416-419, 424, 431, 435.

Precious stone, **I**, 75 (n. 55).

Price relatives (method of), **I**, 152-161.

Price revolution, **I**, 57; **II**, 178, 209, 306, 307, 378, 384, 387, 408, 411-419, 435.

Printer, printing, **II**, 189, 196, 331, 333, 378, 380.

Privilege, the Great Privilege, **II**, 94.

Productivity, **I**, 116 (n. 32), 117 (n. 32); **II**, 117, 168, 170, 293, 295-300, 362, 371, 380, 400, 413, 421, 422.

Proletariat, proletarization, **II**, 196 (n. 299), 198, 378-380.

Prosopographic method, **I**, 39, 42, 43, 139, 142, 149, 477, 507.

Prosperity, **II**, 73, 77, 86, 115, 118, 134-136, 140, 143, 150-153, 166, 173, 176, 180, 187, 191-195, 210, 211, 213, 216, 219, 220, 221 (n. 72), 222, 223, 226 (n. 100), 227-234, 237, 239, 258, 262, 305, 335, 356, 374-376, 381-388, 390, 393, 399, 404, 410, 413-416, 418-420, 424, 429-434.

Protectionism, **II**, 214.

Protestantism, **II**, 235, 258 (n. 99).

Proxy, **II**, 343.

Psychological factor, **II**, 33, 93, 144, 149, 153, 234, 290, 292, 306, 310, 337, 365 (n. 166), 383, 395-397, 414, 418, 435.

Publican, **I**, 294; **II**, 304.

Purchasing power, **I**, 121, 154, 158, 160; **II**, 184, 217, 338 (n. 26), 374, 381 (n. 53), 397; **III**, 90.

Q

Quantitative theory, **I**, 116; **II**, 407, 411.

Quareelsteen, see Brick.

Quicksilver, **II**, 131.

Quintal, see Weights, **I**, 72-79.

R

Raad (Wijde, Breede, Maendagsche Raed), see Council, large town council.

Rain, **I**, 550-562.

Rape, rape-seed, **I**, 245-248; **II**, 298 (n. 41).

Rased measure, see Measures of contents, I, 80-102.

Ravensburger Handelsgesellschaft, II, 76 (n. 91).

Raw material, II, 21, 47, 49, 55, 67, 181, 191, 224, 238, 252, 273, 318, 323, 370, 371, 377, 380 (n. 45), 394, 397, 415 (n. 13), 434.

Real, see Money, I, 107-135.

Reaper, II, 31.

,,Realization", I, 13-15, 20, 488; II, 306, 307.

Recambium, II, 203.

Reformation, 152, 159, 162, 212, 227, 232, 233, 261, 306, 362, 384, 420, 431.

Religionsfrieden, II, 216.

Religious war, II, 232, 318.

Renaissance, II, 76, 120, 362.

Rent, I, 7, 18, 32-38, 138, 160, 161, 179, 477-488, 503-506; II, 28 (n. 146), 65, 66 (n. 24), 85, 93, 95, 104, 114, 116, 117, 132, 134, 135 (n. 126), 139, 145, 161, 162 (n. 116), 168-171, 174, 194, 211, 212, 215, 219, 227, 236, 239, 247, 252, 253, 257, 270, 272, 276, 300, 301 (n. 56), 329, 337 (n. 21), 344 (n. 64), 364, 375, 385, 386, 402 (n. 33), 435; III, 69, 70.

Rent, groundrent, I, 109; II, 61, 65 (n. 21), 117.

Rent, hereditary rent, I, 13, 20, 32, 109; II, 48 (n. 115), 354.

Rent, redeemable rent, I, 34; II, 336, 337, 354, 355 (n. 114), 364.

Rentmeesterbrief II, 204, 243 (n. 217), 355.

Retail price, retail trade, I, 30, 31, 104 (n. 152); II, 132, 324, 334, 335.

Revaluation, I, 112, 123, 125 (n. 52), 126 (n. 54), 127 (n. 56); II, 13, 14-17, 27, 29, 38, 41, 44, 47, 48, 53, 91, 97-99, 109, 114, 119, 159 (n. 107), 163, 167, 200, 228, 233 (n. 149), 262, 383, 429.

Rhine guilder, see Money, I, 107-135; II, 53, 74 (n. 75), 82 (n. 129).

Rhine wine, see Wine.

Roede, see Measures of contents, I, 80-102, and Measures of length and area, I, 102-105.

Rope, rope making, I, 30, 79, 144; II, 227 (n. 115).

Rough oats (*avena strigosa, ruwe evene*), I, 10, 11, 13, 20, 94, 98, 194.

Ruwe evene, see Rough oats.

Rye, I, 6, 7, 9-13, 17-23, 52, 71, 86, 87, 89, 91, 93, 95, 98, 99, 158, 159, 173-182, 497, 498, 534-537, 539-544; II, 32, 110, 115, 116, 171, 174, 213, 218 (n. 54), 246, 250, 253, 261, 282, 381 (n. 53), 391-393, 402, 421; III, 16, 17, 38-59, 116, 117.

S

Sacco di Roma, II, 149.

Sack, see Weights, I, 72-79; see Measures of contents, II, 80-102.

Sack-cloth, I, 273.

Safe-conduct, II, 103 (n. 87), 107.

Saffron, I, 306, 328-331.

Sail-cloth, I, 103, 273-276; II, 89 (n. 4), 176, 183, 224; III, 50, 51.

Sailing technique, II, 327.

Salt, I, 95, 96, 101, 102, 225, 287-293, 535-537; II, 20, 43 (n. 78), 144, 156, 189, 197, 251, 261, 319, 398,

422, 424; **III**, 42, 49, 56, 57, 104, 118.

Salt, Flemish salt, **I**, 102.

Salt, French Bay salt, **I**, 28, 95, 96, 287, 288, 291-293; **II**, 43, 50, 78, 144, 224, 398, 422, 423; **III**, 43, 48.

Salt, *Grand parti du sel*, **II**, 261.

Salt, Iberian salt, **I**, 287, 288; **II**, 261.

Salt, Portuguese salt, **I**, 96.

Salt, Zeeland salt, **I**, 28, 95, 96, 102, 287-290; **II**, 43 (n. 78), 78, 423; **III**, 43.

Salt market, **I**, 287, 288.

Salt pan, **I**, 43 (n. 78).

Salt refining industry, **I**, 96, 287; **II**, 78, 100, 138, 251, 253, 380, 423.

Salt staple, see Staple.

Sample (sale on), **II**, 330.

Sand, shifting sand, **II**, 34, 292.

Satin, **II**, 187, 258.

Sawyer, **I**, 333, 366-377, 457-463.

Say, say industry, **II**, 77, 118, 138, 145, 181, 186, 215, 225, 229, 236, 240, 247, 252, 256, 258, 317 (n. 46), 398, 399; **III**, 61, 106, 107.

Scales of Antwerp (*Waag*), **I**, 75-77; **II**, 133.

Scatter diagram, **I**, 167.

Schelling, see Money, **I**, 107-135.

Schepel, see Measures of contents, **I**, 80-102.

Schmalkaldic war, **II**, 159.

Schuit, see Measures of contents, **I**, 80-102.

Scrupel, see Weights, **I**, 72-79.

Scudo de marchi, see Money, **I**, 107-135; **II**, 367.

Sculpture, **I**, 45, 333; **II**, 133, 226.

Scythe, **II**, 297.

Sea Beggars, **II**, 237, 239, 240, 250-252.

Seasonal fluctuation, **I**, 26, 27, 143,

144, 146, 204, 210; **II**, 401.

Seed, **I**, 98; **II**, 298, 300 (n. 53).

Self-sufficiency, **II**, 289, 291, 293.

Serge, **I**, 54.

Serge drapery, see Drapery.

Serpelier, see Weights, **I**, 72-79.

Servant (maid), **I**, 40, 41, 50, 63, 217 (n. 1); **II**, 303, 304.

Shearer, see Cloth dresser.

Shearers' guild, see Cloth Dressers' guild.

Sheep, **I**, 508; **II**, 31, 34, 62, 64 (n. 19), 115, 210, 211, 248, 298, 304, 372 (n. 13).

Shoe, shoe making, **I**, 29, 533, 538; **II**, 195 (n. 293), 304.

Shoe laces, **II**, 152.

Shopkeeper, **I**, 67; **II**, 234.

Sickle, **II**, 297.

Silk, silk weaving, **I**, 104; **II**, 76 (n. 87), 120, 135 (n. 126), 181, 187, 189, 224, 258, 260 (n. 121), 274, 312 (n. 17).

Silver, **I**, 60, 75 (n. 55), 107-135, 522; **II**, 26, 29, 57 (n. 170), 67, 82, 104, 105, 109, 110, 114, 124, 125, 128, 129, 148, 159, 160, 177, 178, 192, 202, 203, 205, 206, 209, 215-217, 237, 265, 273 (n. 21), 280-282, 309, 311, 316, 317, 321, 343 (n. 60), 367 (n. 178), 376, 409, 411, 412, 414, 416-418, 430; **III**, 26, 27, 38-41, 44, 45, 48, 49, 54-57, 76-78, 118.

Silver currency, **II**, 14, 16, 17, 36, 38 (n. 39), 80, 126, 147, 148, 159 (n. 107), 160, 163, 184, 211, 230, 231, 251, 260, 333 (n. 2), 338, 412.

Silver equivalent, see Money, **I**, 107-135; **II**, 290 (n. 6); **III**, 26, 27, 38-41, 44, 45, 48, 49, 54-57, 76-78, 119.

Sister, see Measures of contents, **I**, 80-102.

Sixt penny (of the feudal host), **II**, 66.

Skipper, **I**, 30; **II**, 77 (n. 94), 132, 133, 274.

Slate-hanger, **I**, 333.

Smoked herring, **I**, 101, 277, 278, 283-287.

Snow, **I**, 550-562.

Soap, soap works, **I**, 79, 81; **II**, 189, 197, 380.

Soapash, **II**, 299 (n. 46).

Solar cycle, **I**, 163 (n. 68).

Spezialization (agricultural), **II**, 170-171, 300-302.

Spezialized industry, see Industry.

Specie-points, **I**, 120.

Speculation, **II**, 107, 109, 124-127, 152, 159, 160, 177, 199, 202, 204, 231, 243 (n. 217), 260, 265, 267, 270, 309-311, 317, 320 (n. 55), 338 (n. 26), 356, 364-366, 409, 412, 414, 431, 434.

Spices, **I**, 72 (n. 41), 73, 79, 114, 146, 148, 226, 306-331, 534-537; **II**, 21, 22, 50, 76, 77, 104, 105, 123-131, 143, 153-157, 161, 273, 317, 319, 320, 337, 395, 398, 403, 424, 431.

Spice trade, **I**, 306; **II**, 22, 76, 78, 104, 124-131, 144, 153-157, 159, 281, 362, 424.

Spijker, **I**, 7.

Spijkermeester, **I**, 13, 14.

Spinner, **I**, 333; **II**, 118, 304, 370 (n. 9).

Spinning, **II**, 89, 118 (n. 23), 293.

Spinning wheel, **II**, 175.

Spiral process, **II**, 34, 418.

Spurry, **II**, 299.

Stamping (of weights and measures), **I**, 67, 68, 80, 82, 90, 94, 257.

Stamping Service, **I**, 80 (n. 73), 84 (n. 87), 90.

Standard deviation, **I**, 165, 167.

Standard of living, **II**, 72 (n. 67), 139, 381-388.

Staple, Alum staple, **II**, 103.

Staple, Grain staple, **II**, 102, 121.

Staple, Wine staple, **I**, 295; **II**, 78 (n. 101), 183.

Staple of Cologne, **I**, 73.

Staple of Dordrecht, **II**, 53, 161 (n. 114).

Staple of English cloth, **II**, 53, 119-123, 229, 230, 237, 431.

Staple of English wool, **II**, 11, 13, 19, 26, 40 (n. 56), 46 (n. 94), 342 (n. 54).

Staple of fats, **II**, 24.

Staple of the Hansa, **II**, 14, 15, 74, 79 (n. 111).

Staple of herring, **I**, 278.

Staple of salt, fish and oats, **I**, 95; **II**, 20, 32.

Staple of Spanish wool, **II**, 131, 179, 330, 378.

States, **II**, 162, 248.

States General, **II**, 86 (n. 149), 94, 214, 245, 246, 248, 264 (n. 155), 265, 277, 355, 366 (n. 171).

States of Brabant, **II**, 94, 211 (n. 7), 220.

States of Flanders, **II**, 162 (n. 122), 269.

Steen, stone, see Weights, **I**, 72-79.

Stock, **II**, 129 (n. 94).

Stone cutter, stone cutting, **I**, 40 (n. 108), 45, 48 (n. 130), 333; **II**, 72, 197, 385 (n. 64), 387 (n. 72).

Stone dealer, **I**, 257.

Stone lime, **I**, 262.

Stoop, see Measures of contents, I, 80-102.

Storm, I, 550-562; II, 54.

Straw, I, 29.

Strettezza, II, 29, 57, 141, 148, 149, 200, 203, 205, 240, 243, 260, 263, 264, 266, 267, 282, 359.

Strike, II, 134, 152, 193, 198, 230.

Stroo, see Measures of contents, I, 80-102.

Strykerye (of Leiden), II, 49 (n. 121); III, 61.

Stuiver, see Money, I, 107-135.

Subsistence minimum, II, 150, 151, 197.

Substitute, II, 390.

Sugar (cane sugar), I, 306, 318-324, 534-537; II, 77, 105, 120, 130, 179, 189, 197, 380, 423, 424; III, 42, 43, 46, 47, 118.

Suit, II, 251.

Surgeon barber, I, 39.

Syrup, I, 81

T

Taflettier, II, 109, 357. 358.

Tailor, II, 135 (n. 126).

Talies, see Measures of length and area I, 102-105.

Tally, I, 26, 31; II, 86, 324, 334-336.

Tanner, I, 242; II, 116.

Tapestry hall, II, 188, 192 (n. 276), 255, 329.

Tapestry weaving, I, 55; II, 70, 71, 118, 135 (n. 127), 138, 181, 188, 196, 226, 255, 276 (n. 39), 304, 329, 380.

Tapestry worker, tapestry weaver, II, 70 (n. 57), 71, 100 (n. 69), 195 (n. 293), 261 (n. 129), 304, 323 (n. 79), 338; III, 63.

Tarras, I, 100, 102; II, 319 (n. 54).

Taswerk, I, 50.

Tax, taxation, I, 54, 55, 59, 75, 76, 228, 510, 529; II, 35 (n. 22), 86, 94-96, 139 (n. 159), 153, 165, 204, 205, 212, 214, 218, 231, 236, 239, 242, 253, 255, 363, 430.

Tax, Crane tax, II, 259, 274.

Tax, Fifth penny tax, II, 255.

Tax, Hundred penny tax, I, 63, 141, 150, 507; II, 175 (n. 177), 255, 304, 307 (n. 86).

Tax, Tenth penny tax, I, 68; II, 204 (n. 350).

Technique, agricultural technique, II, 168, 169 (n. 157), 172, 289, 290, 292, 295-303, 421, 433.

Technique, commercial technique, II, 318, 321, 322, 325, 331, 332, 369, 423, 425, 433.

Technique, financial technique, II, 58, 141, 149, 166, 201, 202, 221, 222, 241, 252, 325 (n. 88), 332-368, 433.

Technique, technical innovation, see Innovation.

Technique, technical skill, II, 72, 81, 94, 129, 135, 189, 195, 196, 238, 279, 375, 378, 379, 434.

Tender, I, 43.

Tenth penny tax, see Tax.

Textile worker, II, 49, 68, 69, 72, 94, 133.

Thatcher, I, 45; II, 387 (n. 72).

Thaw, I, 550-562.

Theology, II, 353, 354.

Thresher, **I**, 333.

Thunderstorm, **I**, 550-562.

Tick weaving, **II**, 118, 138, 190, 259, 375-377.

Tile, **I**, 257.

Timber, see Wood.

Tin, tin worker, **I**, 70, 73, 80.

Tithe, **I**, 51, 52; **II**, 62 (n. 6), 393.

Toll, toll farming, **I**, 58, 141, 510-516; **II**, 37, 39 (n. 41), 46, 54, 56, 84, 123, 141, 144, 145, 204, 218, 230 (n. 134), 310 (n. 8), 327 (n. 99), 341 (n. 47), 396 (n. 22).

Toll, Brabant Land toll, **I**, 55, 59, 65, 510, 517; **II**, 52, 161, 164 (n. 132), 190 (n. 265), 216, 230 (n. 134), 235 (n. 164), 251, 255, 256.

Toll, Brabant transit toll, **II**, 314 (n. 24).

Toll, Brabant Water toll, **I**, 57-59, 510, 511-516; **II**, 27, 39, 56, 57 (n. 170), 61 (n. 2), 70 (n. 55), 75, 84 (n. 142), 100 (n. 71), 102 (n. 81), 122, 123, 144 (n. 4), 166 (n. 148), 177, 182 (n. 213), 240.

Toll, Cattle toll of Lier, **I**, 59; **II**, 210; **III**, 88, 89.

Toll, Freedom of toll, **I**, 58, 60; **II**, 63 (n. 14).

Toll, Great toll on the Zwin, **II**, 77.

Toll, Ridder toll, **I**, 514 (n. 7, 8).

Toll, Sound toll, **I**, 56.

Toll, Tariffs of toll, **I**, 57-60, 84 (n. 85), 109, 510 ; **II**, 50, 224.

Toll, Taxation ad valorem, **I**, 57.

Toll, Toll of Iersekeroord, **II**, 46.

Toll, Toll of Luithagen, **I**, 58 (n. 166).

Toll, Transport toll of Lier, **I**, 59; **II**, 40, 49 (n. 119), 68 (n. 45), 75,

90 (n. 7), 99 (n. 66); **III**, 48, 49, 88, 89.

Toll, Zeeland Water toll, **I**, 57, 59; **II**, 39, 123, 145.

Ton, see Measures of contents, **I**, 80-102.

Tonharing, see Herring.

Tools (agricultural), **II**, 296, 297.

Tower-guard, **I**, 39.

Trade, active long-distance trade, **II**, 11, 19, 26, 44, 52, 54, 55, 73, 74, 131, 136, 191, 222, 238, 252, 253, 257, 263, 274, 277, 309, 315, 321, 322, 326, 339, 378, 412, 416, 425, 429.

Trade, Eastern trade, Baltic trade, **II**, 63, 79, 83, 102, 120, 122, 216, 219, 224, 225, 229, 237, 240, 251, 276, 278, 312-314, 318, 322, 377, 392 (n. 10), 417, 425, 431.

Trade, interregional trade, **II**, 32, 41, 50, 132.

Trade, Levant trade, **II**, 177, 180, 186, 273, 312 (n. 17), 317, 423.

Trade, regional trade, **II**, 19-21, 68 (n. 45), 72 (n. 67), 90, 99, 124, 158, 250, 279, 282, 314, 315, 323, 324, 397, 424.

Trade, Rhine trade, **II**, 39.

Trade, Southern trade, **II**, 143, 177-183, 187, 190, 201, 222, 225, 226, 237, 239, 240, 252, 260 (n. 125), 263, 277 278, 279, 282, 317, 322, 363, 377, 416, 431.

Trade, transcontinental overland trade, **II**, 18, 20, 26, 51, 52, 55, 59, 76, 77, 83, 104, 119, 124, 128, 130, 131, 136, 143, 145, 156, 157, 181, 186, 224, 237, 238, 251 (n. 51), 256, 279, 289, 291, 295, 309-312, 314-318, 321, 326-328, 369, 370, 408, 423, 424, 429-431, 433, 435.

Trade, maritime trade, **II**, 19, 21, 50, 76-78, 102, 105, 120, 123, 124, 130, 136, 144, 157, 159 (n. 106), 166, 171, 172, 177, 179, 191, 211, 213, 216-219, 223, 237-240, 246, 250-254, 259, 282, 291, 311-313, 315-318, 321, 322, 326-328, 331, 369, 390, 392, 398, 408, 412, 423, 424, 429, 433, 434, 435.

Trade, transit trade, **I**, 23 (n. 61), 59; **II**, 22 (n. 109), 25, 26, 46, 47, 52-54, 74, 75, 82, 83, 104, 114, 120, 121, 125, 143, 145 (n. 9), 156, 158, 177, 184, 186, 216-219, 225, 230, 238, 257, 309 (n. 4), 314, 315, 398, 412, 414, 423, 430; **III**, 61, 106.

Transport, **II**, 34 (n. 19), 40, 128, 157, 161, 181, 217, 246, 321, 327, 328, 378, 380, 390, 429.

Transport cost, see Cost of transport.

Treasurers' bill, see *Rentmeestersbrief*.

Treaty, see Peace.

Trend method, **I**, 161-164; **III**, 28, 29.

Troy weight, see Mark weight.

Truce, Twelve Years' truce, **II**, 272, 277.

Truce of Vaucelles, **II**, 213, 214.

Trunk making, see Coffer making.

Turba, **II**, 343.

Turnip, turnip bread, **II**, 116, 168, 299.

Turve, **I**, 95, 100.

Typology of the crisis, **II**, 389-406, 415 (n. 12).

Type founder, **II**, 226.

U

Unemployment, **II**, 15, 17, 48 (n. 115), 49, 90, 96-98, 150, 162, 229, 230, 231 (n. 136), 232, 236, 240, 242, 290, 296 (n. 33), 378, 383, 387, 400, 404, 419, 420, 430.

University of Louvain, **II**, 70.

Undervaluation, **II**, 36, 82, 148.

Urbanization, **II**, 8, 192, 193.

Vaert, see Measures of contents, **I**, 80-102.

Vat, see Weights, **I**, 72-79; see Measures of contents, **I**, 80-102.

Vegetables, **I**, 533, 535-537; **II**, 293, 385.

Velocity of money circulation, **II**, 363 (n. 151), 412.

Verdiering, **I**, 477.

Vetch, **I**, 98.

Viertel, see Measures of contents, **I**, 80-102.

Villeinage, **II**, 291, 295 (n. 31), 302 (n. 65).

Vinager, **I**, 28, 81, 535, 537; **III**, 24, 25.

Vineyard, **I**, 294, 295; **II**, 301 (n. 56).

Viticulture, **I**, 295; **II**, 63, 300, 301.

Waelpot, see Measures of contents, **I**, 80-102.

Wage, see Weights, **I**, 72-79.

Wage differentiation, **I**, 334; **II**, 196, 279, 379, 388, 434.

Wage tariff, **II**, 134, 194, 211 (n. 7), 228 (n. 120), 275-277, 279 (n. 58), 374, 403.

Waterland, see polder.

Wax, **I**, 73, 79, 300-305; **II**, 63, 158, 301; **III**, 48, 49.

Weather, **I**, 164 (n. 73), 549-562; **II**, 8, 33, 36, 89, 96, 114, 115, 167, 213, 231, 246, 250, 260, 271

167

(n. 15), 277, 332, 390, 398, 414 (n. 9).

Weaver, I, 41, 55, 149; II, 9-11, 16, 17, 18 (n. 88), 33 (n. 9), 42, 44, 68, 98, 99 (n. 63), 118, 152, 164, 187, 193, 303, 304, 323 (n. 80), 335, 370 (n. 3), 382, 405; III, 62.

Weighing coefficient, I, 147, 155, 158, 164.

Weight of bread, I, 6, 7, 13, 14, 20, 23, 66, 93, 183; III, 14.

Wheat, I, 6, 7, 13, 16, 19, 21, 22, (n. 56), 24 (n. 61), 29, 52, 98, 146, 147, 151, 152, 183-188; II, 32, 192, 298 (n. 42), 313 (n. 21), 392, 393, 405; III, 14-17, 29, 96, 114, 115.

Wholesale price, wholesale trade, I, 30, 31, 76 (n. 60); II, 324 (n. 84).

Wind, I, 550-562.

Wine, I 28-30, 60, 61, 67, 80, 82-84 (n. 86), 145 (n. 18), 148, 510, 520, 534-537; II, 14, 86, 249, 300, 301, 319, 324, 330, 395, 403; III, 24, 25, 49, 64.

Wine, Alsace wine, II, 63.

Wine, Brabant wine, country wine (lantwijn), I, 83, 296; II, 64, 300, 301.

Wine, French wine, I, 83, 84, 294, 295; II, 63, 183, 320 (n. 58).

Wine, Mediterranean wine, I, 84.

Wine, Rhine wine, I, 30 (n. 73), 83, 84, 294-299; II, 54 (n. 153), 63, 64 (n. 16), 183, 320 (n. 58), 395, 398, 424; III, 42, 43, 48, 104, 118.

Wine trade, I, 295; II, 52, 54 (n. 153), 63, 183 (n. 221).

Wijde Raed, see Great council.

Wis, see Measures of contents, I, 80-102.

Witte evene, see Oats.

Wood, see Firewood.

Wood (forest), I, 38, 45, 238, 242, 254, 447, 489-492; II, 116, 118, 168, 174, 175 (n. 175), 176, 211, 246, 299, 303, 304, 305 (n. 79), 319 (n. 54), 397, 412, 415.

Wood (timber), II, 189, 327, 330.

Wood carving, wood cutting, I, 238; II, 70, 116, 175 (n. 177), 188, 193, 246 (n. 7), 304.

Wood gatherer, I, 238; II, 116, 304.

Wool, I, 79; II, 10, 21, 22, 27, 42, 46, 47 (n. 109), 48, 68, 110, 180, 210, 278, 304, 319 (n. 54), 337 (n. 23), 369 (n. 3), 371, 372, 373; III, 63.

Wool, Eastern wool, I, 59, 65.

Wool, English wool, I, 79; II, 11, 13, 19, 22 (n. 109), 26, 27, 31, 34 (n. 19), 40 (n. 56), 46, 47, 49, 62, 67, 68, 310, 314, 371, 372, 378.

Wool, native wool, II, 67, 210 (n. 6), 319 (n. 54), 372.

Wool, Spanish wool, I, 58, 65, 79; II, 67, 131, 136, 178, 180, 187, 223, 224, 235, 281, 330 (n. 112), 338, 372, 378.

Wüstungen, II, 291, 292, 296 (n. 32), 413.

Yke, Yking, I, 80.

Zunftzwang, II, 68.

(B 120-3)   Imprimerie Ceuterick, s.c., rue de Bruxelles 153, Louvain
Dir. L. Pitsi, rue Dagobert 25, Louvain (Belgique)